NORMAN PERRIN'S INTERPRETATION OF THE NEW TESTAMENT

Norman Perrin, mid-60s
Photo courtesy of the Divinity School,
The University of Chicago

Studies in American Biblical Hermeneutics 2

NORMAN PERRIN'S INTERPRETATION OF THE NEW TESTAMENT

*From "Exegetical Method"
to "Hermeneutical Process"*

by
C A L V I N   R .   M E R C E R

MERCER

ISBN 0-86554-219-8

The paper used in this publication
meets the minimum requirements of American National
Standard for Information Sciences—Permanence of Paper
for Printed Library Materials, ANSI Z39.48-1984.

Library of Congress Cataloging-in-Publication Data
Mercer, Calvin R.
Norman Perrin's interpretation of the New Testament.

(Studies in American biblical hermeneutics ; 2)
Bibliography: p. 119.
Includes indexes.
1. Perrin, Norman—Contributions in New Testament
exegesis. 2. Bible. N.T.—Criticism, interpretation,
etc.—History—20th century. I. Title. II. Series.
BS2350.M47   1986   225.6'092'4   86-28510
ISBN 0-86554-219-8 (alk. paper)

··CONTENTS··

•EDITOR'S PREFACE•

Why a series entitled "American Biblical Hermeneutics?" Why not "American Theology," for example, or simply "Biblical Hermeneutics?" These are complex questions that require a multidimensional response. To begin, the very terminology "American biblical hermeneutics" is intrinsically interdisciplinary and pluralistic. That fact alone establishes an important foundation for this field of study. In whatever way we may conceive and think about American biblical hermeneutics, it can only be approached dialectically. The path to the revitalization of the Christian tradition in our time requires cross-disciplined stimulation. Norman Perrin recognized this, as have all formative biblical interpreters in the modern context. In this sense *American biblical hermeneutics implies a redirecting of the critical approach to biblical texts back upon the readers of those same texts.* It has sympathies with contemporary "reader response" criticism in that it requires a critical working through of the act of reading itself. As recent studies have shown, there are various strategies in the reading process, just as there are various strategies built into the writing process. The more explicit these strategies are revealed, the more opportunity for a meaningful reading experience. The way that such strategies are operative in Perrin's influential contribution to the reading of the New Testament in the American setting helps us better understand where we are today in reading the Bible and where we might go from here.

A significant problem for hermeneutics in our day lies in its becoming an intellectual end in itself. As a result, "American biblical hermeneutics" begins, ends, and also continually maintains the dialectic between our cultural texts and biblical texts. The danger of erecting an imposing theoretical structure that actually *obstructs* the creative development of knowledge is arguably more of a danger in hermeneutics than in most other academic disciplines because this intellectual activity can so easily rob us of the intimacy of primary texts. As always, as a safeguard and source of vitality, theory must be wedded to practically—in this case, the continued reading of those primary texts. One of the major reasons that Perrin's work is central for understanding biblical hermeneutics in our time and place is that his hermeneutics grows organically out of his exegesis of the New Testament. In what other biblical interpreter of our time on the American scene do we see a greater ongoing vitality in the components that make for creative scholarship—the continued force of the received continental traditions and a rethinking of those traditions within the intellectual life of the new American setting, activities set in the context of a continued rigorous reading of New Testament texts themselves? In such a confluence of intellectual forces in the mind of a single figure, we gain a rare glimpse of the birthing of an American biblical hermeneutics.

Philosophically, "American biblical hermeneutics" implies the priority of particularity over universality in theological discourse. The Christian church has traditionally interpreted itself in universal terms, but this is a universality that is grounded in the particularities of its religious faith, particularities that are themselves grounded in cultural existence. All too frequently American ecclesiastical institutions have not inquired into the fundamentals of American thought in their theological formulations. But to bypass the cultural component in religious reflection means ultimately to deny our common human flesh, and flesh seems to have a way of maintaining its integrity and hold on us regardless of our pretensions. Taking these factors into consideration, it has become clear that the American cultural context demands a dynamic perception of the Bible that does not merely predicate absolutes about God based on this or that biblical text, but recognizes that any "uncovering" of truth always assumes a particular shape and form subject to the delimitations of the cultural matrix of the "one-to-whom-is-revealed." The biblical text itself *requires* that each individual reader bring the totality of her or his life experience to the task of reading. Laying bare the principles of our interpretive efforts represents a complement to the interdisciplinary considerations noted above and will aid us in the restoration of the vitality of the Bible in *both* our ecclesiastical and cultural life. In order for this to happen, American biblical hermeneutics must be conceived in such a way as to manifest and nurture those fundamental theological ties that exist between the life of the reader, and the life of the biblical text.

Biblical hermeneutics takes an important step beyond specific issues of biblical criticism and inquires into the ways that these biblical experiences are relevant to the contemporary experience of the text. What is the theological payoff of such experiences for the modern experience? How does one translate perspectives and concerns that are out of date? How does one move profitably from contemporary problematic experiences to the world of the text in which such experiences were nonexistent? Such an approach to the Bible is fully human, yet does not fracture the vitality of the religious experience itself. Rather, it is an approach that is open and searching: it is "acanonical" in the sense that it requires the experience of the reader to *complement* the experience of the biblical author *prior to* the establishment of theological discourse. Moreover, it is worked out in the knowledge that the subjective concerns of faith from generation to generation are formative in the producton of biblical texts. Therefore, the interpretation of American religious experience must be set in the context of the broader American cultural experience, if it is to follow the full implications of the challenge that is in the Bible itself. This fact is not determined by theological preference or predilection for things American. It is the simple acknowledgment of *what must be the case when we allow the fuller meaning of the biblical texts to penetrate our own thinking.* As this work shows, Perrin, as European-born and educated reader of the Bible in the American context, fully recognized and manifested this insight in his work. As such, he presents us with an unusual opportunity of seeing how this entire process may actually work. This is the general starting point for all reflection on the scope and character of American biblical hermeneutics.

Perrin's first-hand training in the literary-critical methods of biblical study developed in Europe particularly sensitized him to the fresh models of literary criticism operative in the American setting. Above all, one sees the impact of the so-called American New Criticism that is examined in this book. Certainly Perrin was far from an exegetical "ideologue" who attempted simply to impress his adopted culture with what had "worked" with so much success abroad. If he had chosen this easier route, he would not have been a fit figure for study in this series. Rather, he captured the dialectical essence of American pluralism. As he rightly saw it, the task was not to turn one's back on the European traditions, but to bring them into dialogue with the new American setting. What Perrin embodied in his own life remains as a theological challenge to those of us who have appropriated European methodological and theological traditions in a more vicarious way. Why does such a study belong to hermeneutics, and not simply to the history of biblical interpretation? Because Perrin's intellectual odyssey is one that featured the breaking of contemporary ideologies of biblical criticism—even if that ideology be formulated on the well-traversed thoroughfares of European historical and literary biblical criticis. Implied here is the recognition that even the true must change and be renewed in order to remain the true. Historically, Christianity has made its greatest impact in the European context, a situation rooted in the phenomenal growth of Hellenistic Gentile Christianity in the first century of the Common Era. But Perrin correctly shows us that Christianity *as such* is decidedly *not* simply a European religion. At the heart of its most theoretical formulations, Christian thought must be dialectical or relational, lest it cease to be religion and assume yet another manifestation of twentieth century ideologies. Thus, while it is true that by and large Christianity has been mediated to America through Europe, such mediation is rightly understood as the starting point for our religious reflection, and not the end. It is to be hoped that the heritage of Norman Perrin's reading of the New Testament will help invigorate that reflection. It is to that end that this book is offered as a contribution to this new series "Studies in American Biblical Hermeneutics."

Charles Mabee
Marshall University
10 February 1986

•ACKNOWLEDGMENTS•

I am pleased that the tenth anniversary of Norman Perrin's unexpected death will be marked by the publication of my attempt to take stock of certain strands of his intellectual pilgrimage and to suggest how his long labor on the Jesus tradition can forward the notion of American biblical hermeneutics.

While the final responsibility for this study lies with the author, several persons have in various ways made important contributions that made the process easier and the result better.

I thank Charles Mabee for inaugurating the timely "Studies in American Biblical Hermeneutics" series with his fine book, *Reimagining America*, and for seeing the possibilities that an intellectual biography of Perrin could hold for the series. David Abernathy, close friend and student of Perrin, whose own *Understanding the Teaching of Jesus* is a valuable contribution to our acquaintance with the early part of Perrin's scholarly pilgrimage, took a keen interest in the project from the first day he learned of it. His many letters and our conversations about Perrin's lifework, not to mention his steady encouragement, have been absolutely invaluable.

Other readers of various portions and drafts of the manuscript include Donald E. Cook, David Levenson, Michael Pelt, Robert Price, John Priest, and referees selected by Mercer University Press. Although I was primarily concerned with Perrin's published work, I rounded out the study by seeking access to the Perrin "oral tradition." Acknowledgments to a number of his friends, colleagues, and students who helped along this line are made in the notes.

At East Carolina University, Vice-Chancellor Angelo Volpe and Dean Eugene Ryan gave me generous support as I put the manuscript in final form. I am also grateful to my chairman, James L. Smith, for his significant encouragement. Lora Ehlbeck typed the manuscript with considerable speed and accuracy. Finally, I thank the staff of Mercer University Press for their fine work in producing this book.

To M A R I L Y N

·INTRODUCTION·

At the time of his death in 1976 Norman Perrin was one of the most creative and influential New Testament scholars in post-World War II America. One of the more interesting features of his scholarly pilgrimage is that he changed his mind a number of times about a number of issues. This study provides a critical analysis of his work by uncovering some of the factors behind those changes and by setting his work in the context of modern New Testament scholarship.[1] His creative impulse will serve as an impetus for forwarding the development of an American biblical hermeneutic.

Throughout his pilgrimage Perrin made several distinct, though related, shifts in his choice of exegetical method and his theological conclusions derived from the applicaton of those methods. This study will demonstrate that the fundamental issue he dealt with throughout his work was that of proper method in exegesis of the New Testament and that the

---

[1]No major attempt has yet been made to trace in depth the development of Perrin's work or to assess his contributions to scholarship. Three studies do merit mention at this point. The first, Hans Dieter Betz, ed., *Christology and a Modern Pilgrimage: A Discussion with Norman Perrin* (Claremont: Scholar's Press, 1971), is a collection of essays dealing with Perrin's major publications on Christology. The second is Welton O. Seal, Jr., "The Parousia in Mark: A Debate With Norman Perrin and His School" (1982). This Ph.D. thesis, completed under the direction of Raymond Brown at Union Theological Seminary in New York, is an attempt to call into question the interpretation of the parousia in Mark set forth by Perrin and his students. Finally, the *Journal of Religion*, the University of Chicago publication to which Perrin made many contributions, published a memorial issue in October 1984. Edited by two of Perrin's students, Werner H. Kelber and John R. Donahue, it contains among others, essays on the overall work of Perrin (Kelber), his discussion of the Kingdom of God (Dennis C. Duling), and his discussion of the historical Jesus (Erich Grässer). In addition, it contains an important, heretofore unpublished, paper by Perrin.

underlying theological motive for his work was his quest for a foundation for faith.

Furthermore, this study will demonstrate a reciprocal causative relationship between the exegetical methods used and the theological conclusions derived from the application of those methods. Perrin's scholarly development followed a pattern in which his theology sought support from a method that when applied, led to conclusions that necessitated a shift in theology. The cycle would then begin again as the new theological postion sought support from a new method. This pattern continued through four shifts of method (conservative form criticism, radical form criticism, redaction criticism, and literary criticism) and corresponding shifts in theology. The shifts in his theology moved Perrin from a position where he viewed history as the basis for faith and toward a position where history was not important for faith. Yet while he was moving *toward* an ahistorical perspective, he never reached it. In addition, there are indications that near the end of his career he was begining to develop an inclusive hermeneutical and theological stance that would incorporate the several emphases of his scholarly pilgrimage.

Intertwined with the internal interplay between method and theology and, of course, external scholarly influences, were two other factors. The first, and more personal, was Perrin's tremendous ambition, a drive to succeed that consistently surfaced in his attempt to work at the forefront of New Testament scholarship. The second was his propensity, once he had adopted an exegetical method, to take the application of that method to an extreme conclusion. This extremist solution to a number of New Testament problems was his way of achieving a kind of order, logic, and clarity in his research and writing.

As Patrick Henry pointed out, it is healthy for a discipline to be aware of where it is, how it arrived there, and where it might be going.[2] A study of Perrin's work can be especially helpful to those interested in such questions with respect to New Testament studies, for that work is paradigmatic of certain crucial issues in modern New Testament scholarship. Perrin was particularly interested in proper exegetical method and he moved through several of the major methods utilized by New Testament scholars. In addition, his work reflects the diverse interpretations of the relationship between faith and history that one finds among students of the New Testament in the modern era. While he did substantial work on the Son of man issue and the Gospel of Mark, this study will focus only on his interpretation of the Kingdom of God and parables. It is with these aspects of the teaching of Jesus that one can most readily chart his methodological and theological pilgrimage and especially his literary turn in the American reformulation.

---

[2]Patrick Henry, *New Directions in New Testament Study* (Philadelphia: Westminster Press, 1979) 17.

Perrin died in 1976 following a relatively short but productive career as a New Testament scholar.[3] His literary output included 30 articles and eight books.[4] Because he shifted his position on important issues several times, it will be helpful to provide a brief sketch of his life. This biographical sketch highlights his professional life as an educator and author and takes special note of his scholarly environment at particular times in his career.

Perrin was born the son of a mill worker on 29 November 1920, in Wellingborough, Northamptonshire, England. His parents, as was often the case in British society, expected him to continue in the class of his birth. By grammer school, though, it was evident that young Perrin was an intellectually gifted student. Military service in the intelligence branch of the Royal Air Force from 1940 to 1945 gave him the opportunity to see beyond the confines of his working class background and the determination to move beyond it. Those who knew him well later in his life spoke of his being motivated by an intense drive and ambition to succeed. This was due, at least in part, to his earnest desire to repudiate his background by excelling in his profession—he called this "making it."[5] This deter-

---

[3]Unless otherwise indicated, the biographical data in this study will be taken from "A Memorial Tribute to Norman Perrin: 1920-1976," *Criterion* 16 (Winter 1977); and from interviews in the summer of 1983 with his former colleagues and students. Those interviewed include David Abernathy, former adjunct professor, Candler School of Theology, Emory University, Atlanta, Georgia; Hendrikus Boers, professor of New Testament, Candler School of Theology; John R. Donahue, professor of New Testament, Jesuit School of Theology, Berkeley, California; Dennis C. Duling, associate professor, Reigious Studies Department, Canisius College, New York, New York; Manfred Hoffmann, professor of church history and historical theology, Candler School of Theology; Werner H. Kelber, Isla and Percy Turner Professor of Religious Studies, Rice University, Houston, Texas; Theodore H. Runyon, Jr., professor of Systematic Theology, Candler School of Theology; Mary Ann Tolbert, associate professor of New Testament and Early Christianity, The Divinity School, Vanderbilt University, Nashville, Tennessee; and Theodore R. Weber, professor of Social Ethics, Candler School of Theology. See also the reminiscence of David Abernathy, Perrin's student, friend, and colleague, in *Understanding the Teaching of Jesus* (New York: Seabury Press, 1983) 200-202. *Understanding the Teaching of Jesus* is based on a series of lectures Perrin recorded privately for laypersons in 1962.

[4]In addition to his books and articles Perrin wrote nearly forty book reviews and translated into English five works by Joachim Jeremias, with whom he studied in Germany. See the bibliography for a list of Perrin's publications.

[5]In one of the contributions to the "Memorial Tribute" (8), Brian Gerrish recalls an incident illustrative of Perrin's desire to succeed: "Some time ago, after we had been present together at the memorial of a common friend, he told me the kind of requiem he would choose for *himself*. It might not be thought quite proper if I shared with you the whole of his impromptu liturgy; but it ended with the words: 'While he was here, he made quite a splash.' "

mination to succeed was later manifested in his continuing attempt to work on the cutting edge of New Testament scholarship.

After returning from service, Perrin entered Manchester University as a divinity student and received a Bachelor of Arts degree in 1949. At Manchester he came under the scholarly influence of T. W. Manson, about whom he later spoke with high regard. Manson's conservative approach to the New Testament involved a respect for the historicity of the synoptic tradition and a conviction that the historical Jesus provided the foundation for faith, two judgments that later surfaced in Perrin's work.

After graduation Perrin married Rosemary Watson, a middle-class lady who, unlike his parents, encouraged him in his academic pursuits and reinforced his drive to succeed. He enrolled in London University, where he received the Bachelor of Divinity (with honors) in 1952 and the Master of Theology (in Greek New Testament and Apocrypha studies) in 1956. The London period was a time when Perrin equipped himself with some of the more technical knowledge necessary for expertise in New Testament studies. He immersed himself in the Greek New Testament and continued his study of languages, particularly German, which he had begun during his military career.

In 1949 Perrin was ordained to the ministry of the Baptist Union of Great Britain and Northern Ireland, and he engaged in a brief ecclesiastical career while a graduate student at London University.[6] It has been noted, however, that he became less interested in the institutional church as he increasingly absorbed himself in scholarly research.

By the time he was completing his work at London, Perrin had realized that the road to recognition in the New Testament field involved a close knowledge of the German scene. With financial assistance from a number of scholarships and awards,[7] he studied from 1956 to 1959 at the University of Göttingen under Joachim Jeremias, the next major scholarly influence on his thinking after Manson. In 1959 he received the Doctor of Theology degree with a dissertation on the Kingdom of God in the teaching of Jesus. Perrin's association with Jeremias reinforced his English heritage. Although his particular interests were somewhat different, Jeremias, like Manson, had a high respect for the historicity of the synoptic tradition and saw the historical Jesus as being in some real sense the object of faith.

Through his contacts with American scholars at Göttingen, particularly Theodore H. Runyon, Jr., who still teaches systematic theology at

---

[6]Perrin served pastorates in the Westbourne Park Baptist Church in London from 1949-1952 and in the Sketty Baptist Church in Swansea, South Wales, from 1952-1956.

[7]Perrin's academic awards included the World Council of Churches Scholarship (1956-1957), Dr. Williams's Traveling Award (1957-1958), and the Alexander von Humboldt Stiftung Stipendiat (1957-1959).

Emory University, Perrin received an invitation to teach at Emory. James M. Robinson, a former professor at Emory and visiting professor at Göttingen when Perrin was a student there, had read in draft form the German version of Perrin's dissertation and was able to add credence to the judgment of Runyon, whose field was theology. From 1959 to 1964 Perrin served first as assistant professor and then associate professor of New Testament at Emory's Candler School of Theology.

He was especially pleased at the chance to teach in America. He knew his opportunities to "make it" in England were practicaly nil, given his working-class background and the concomitant lack of social standing and sophistication; few positions were open in England, anyway. A post in Germany was just as difficult to obtain since he was not German, Lutheran, or Roman Catholic, and since his dissertation had yet to be published. Indeed America became the "land of opportunity," providing him with the chance to develop a scholarly reputation and thereby move upward in the academic world. For Perrin the five years at Emory were characterized by vigorous discussions of questions raised by Rudolf Bultmann, much research, and some publication.

Among the Candler School of Theology faculty members there was a considerable amount of lively discussion, both in private and public forums, on the kerygma and history issue raised by Bultmann. Like many of his colleagues, Perrin became increasingly amenable to Bultmann's perspective. During his stay at Emory, he had good rapport with Thomas J. J. Altizer, around whom the "death-of-God" controversy later swirled. It is safe to assume that the general milieu that fostered the "death-of-God" contributed to Perrin's embrace of Bultmann's perspective.

His desire to win a name for himself in the discipline, combined with a feeling that he had lost several years in the war,[8] drove him to work very hard in his research. His first article, published in the winter of 1959 to 1960 with William R. Farmer, bore witness to his conservative leanings as well as to his increasing acquaintance with (and, at this time, criticism of) the theological perspective of Bultmann. While at Emory he worked from 1959 to 1961 to revise his dissertation, eventually published as *The Kingdom of God in the Teaching of Jesus*.[9] This book was dedicated to the two teachers who up to that time had exercised the most influence on his academic life—Manson and Jeremias. In addition to revising his dissertation, Perrin concentrated his research on the Son of man in the synoptic gospels·from 1961-1964.[10]

---

[8]Perrin was 39 years old when he completed his doctorate and accepted the Emory appointment.

[9]Perrin, *The Kingdom of God in the Teaching of Jesus* (London: SCM Press; Philadelphia: Westminster Press, 1963).

[10]Perrin, "The Contours of a Pilgrimage," in *A Modern Pilgrimage in New Testament Christology* (Philadelphia: Fortress Press, 1974) 2.

In 1964 Perrin was appointed to the post of associate professor of New Testament at the University of Chicago Divinity School. In July 1969 he was promoted to full professor.[11] This appointment came primarily as a result of the positive reception at Chicago of his first book, *Kingdom of God*.[12] Other factors in his favor were an invitation by SCM Press to do a "full-scale treatment of the teaching of Jesus"[13] and his study in Germany under Jeremias, a noted scholar.

Perrin reveled in what he called the "big time" and the opportunity it offered to establish himself more firmly as a scholar by concentrating on research, writing, and directing doctoral students.[14] While at Chicago he advised a number of graduate students whose dissertatons and later publications supported and extended their teacher's work and in many cases forged into new territory. He also became more visible in the Society of Biblical Literature. He was active in the Society's Seminar on the Parables and served as president of the Chicago Society in 1971-1972 and as president of the national Society in 1972-1973.[15]

After his arrival at Chicago, Perrin's publications mushroomed. Several articles from his earlier Son of man studies were published between 1965 and 1968. From 1964 to 1966 he worked intensely on the teaching of Jesus for the book that SCM Press had invited him to write.[16] That book, for which he is perhaps best known, was published in 1967 as *Rediscovering the Teaching of Jesus*.[17] It summarized his solution to the Son of man problem, reflected his continued interest in the Kingdom of God, and

---

[11]Perrin later also became a member of the department of Christian Theology at the Divinity School.

[12]See Jerald C. Brauer in "Memorial Tribute," 13.

[13]Perrin, "Contours," 1.

[14]Perrin's friends recall his excitement at the prospects Chicago offered for developing his reputation as a scholar. He spoke of the relatively lighter teaching load, unlimited secretarial help, and generous funds for travel and for doctoral student fellowships. Emory's Ph.D. program in religion, inaugurated in 1958, was only in its infancy during Perrin's stay there. The emphasis at Candler was still to a large degree on teaching and Perrin was ever frustrated at his limited opportunity to do research and to write.

[15]Perrin also received the Christian Research Foundation Prize for Research in Christian Origins in 1965, and the John Simon Guggenheim Memorial Foundation Fellowship for 1969-1970.

[16]Perrin, "Contours," 1, 6.

[17]Norman Perrin, *Rediscovering the Teaching of Jesus* (London: SCM Press; New York: Harper and Row, 1967). This work was well received in both English and German. The German edition is *Was lehrte Jesus wirklich? Rekonstruktion und Deutung*, trans. P. Nohl (Göttingen: Vandenhoeck und Ruprecht, 1972). The 1976 English edition, in paperback, added a preface.

contained his first major statement on the parables. Along with *The Promise of Bultmann*,[18] his introduction to Bultmann's theology, *Rediscovering* reflected the first major shift in Perrin's approach to the New Testament. Perrin had now moved away from the conservatism he had inherited from Manson and Jeremias to what was essentially a full acceptance of the method (radical form criticism) and theological perspective of Bultmann. According to his wife Nancy, Perrin considered Bultmann to be "the greatest New Testament scholar of the twentieth century, and perhaps the greatest of any century."[19]

The next shift in Perrin's work, one that again placed him at the forefront of research, had already begun. His Son of man studies had led him to Mark's contribution to that tradition and this, among other things to be considered later, led him to adopt redaction criticism. His exposition of this method, which popularized redaction criticism in America, was published as *What is Redaction Criticism?*, the second volume of a series on exegetical methods.[20] Several redaction-critical articles concerned with the interpretation of the Gospel of Mark were published in 1971-1972. Certainly worthy of mention is Perrin's introductory textbook, which contained an extensive chapter on Mark that summarized his work on that Gospel.[21]

Perrin's last major scholarly work was *Jesus and the Language of the Kingdom*.[22] Although there were certainly connections with his earlier work, he here forged beyond his British/German conservative heritage and even beyond the influence of Bultmann. Dedicated to Amos Wilder and Paul Ricoeur, this book reflected a uniquely American influence. Wilder was a predecessor of Perrin at Chicago and a member of the Society of Biblical Literature Seminar on the Parables. Ricoeur, also a Divinity School professor, and Perrin once team-taught a course on the hermeneutics of religious language.[23] Perrin's work in this period also reflected a more sophisticated understanding of myth than that of Bultmann. This was due in part to the influence of Perrin's colleague, Mircea Eliade, who taught

---

[18]Perrin, *The Promise of Bultmann: The Promise of Theology*, ed. Martin E. Marty (Philadelphia J.B. Lippincott, 1969; reprint, Philadelphia: Fortress Press, 1979).

[19]Nancy Perrin, in her foreword to the 1979 Fortress Press reprint of *Promise of Bultmann*, 4.

[20]Perrin, *What is Redaction Criticism* (Philadelphia: Fortress Press, 1969).

[21]Perrin, *The New Testament: An Introduction—Proclamation and Parenesis, Myth and History* (New York: Harcourt Brace Jovanovich, 1974). An edition revised by Dennis Duling, was issued in 1982.

[22]Perrin, *Jesus and the Language of the Kingdom: Symbol and Metaphor in New Testament Interpretation* (Philadelphia: Fortress, 1976).

[23]Ibid., xiii.

in the history of religions field.[24] Perrin's continuing interests in the Kingdom of God, parables, and exegetical method all found expression in *Language*. They were, however, dealt with from the perspective of a literary-critical approach informed by the American New Critical movement.

Although his literary criticism seemed to be moving toward an ahistorical perspective, Perrin considered himself a historian to the end of his life. He saw literary criticism as a corrective to the emphasis on a historical approach that had dominated much of modern biblical study. His goal was to create a new methodological and theological sythesis that would take into account factors he had come to see as important, namely history, theology, and literature. Ultimately, at his retirement, he planned to consummate this synthesis in a theology of the New Testament, something he considered to be the crowning accomplishment of a creative New Testament scholar. He hoped that this theology of the New Testament, along with the "Perrin school" that would result from his work with graduate students,[25] would establish him even further as a leading interpreter of the New Testament.

Perrin underwent major surgery for removal of a kidney in 1969. Even as he recovered, he knew that a malignancy remained in his one good kidney. He was faced with the choice between having another operation that would have cured him but left him practically bed-ridden, or not having surgery and living with the constant threat of death. He chose not to have the operation so he could continue his academic career; and he did with fervor. It is somewhat ironic that the malignancy was not the eventual cause of death. He died unexpectedly of a heart attack on Thanksgiving morning, 25 November 1976, just four days before his fifty-sixth birthday.

In his seventeen-year career, Norman Perrin had the drive, flexibility, and foresight to work on and make important contributions to the constantly changing cutting edge of New Testament scholarship. Toward the end of his career he was creating a brilliant synthesis of the best of European and American thought. Perrin began his scholarly pilgrimage with an accepted exegetical method (form criticism), influenced by a conservative British and German theological perspective. He moved to redac-

---

[24]Perrin's last book, *The Resurrection According to Matthew, Mark, and Luke* (Philadelphia: Fortress Press, 1977), published posthumously, was dedicated to "Mircea Eliade who first taught me that there was more to myth than the instant need to demythologize." This book was published in the United Kingdom as *The Resurrection Narrative: A New Approach* (London: SCM Press, 1977).

[25]See Seal, "Parousia in Mark," 5-9, for the contention that it is appropriate to speak of a Perrin "school." According to Seal (9) the school has produced "a body of scholarship with numerous and clearly defined lines of interconnection and development." The focus of Seal's study, however, was on those students who have concerned themselves primarily with the Gospel of Mark.

tion criticism and then literary criticism, with corresponding theological positions evolving along the way. He did not, however, simply move blindly with the latest fad in theology or exegetical method. Rather, he made careful and appropriate transitions based on solid research, serious dialogue with other scholars, and his own methodological and theological shifts. He jumped on the scholarly bandwagon, not blindly so, but with an accurate perception of trends in scholarship and the ability and determination to contribute to them. Our task is to continue probing those issues his timely work so acutely raises.

Dennis Duling, a student of Perrin who revised Perrin's introduction to the New Testament, commented that "Perrin had moved through several stages in his scholarly career."[26] Perrin himself spoke of his work on the Christology of the New Testament as a "pilgrimage."[27] I have delineated the several stages in his scholarly career, and I suggest that his pilgrimage is best interpreted in terms of the two major issues of exegetical method and the relationship of faith and history.

While the underlying issue Perrin dealt with explicitly throughout his work was that of proper method in exegesis of the New Testament, he was not always clear about the motivation for his work. I will show that the underlying motivation was his quest for an adequate basis for faith. His work can be broadly observed along a continuum where he moved toward a position in which history was less and less important for faith. More specifically, I will demonstrate that there was a reciprocal causative relationship between the various methods of exegesis he utilized and the conclusions he reached as a result of using those methods. These conclusions fostered a movement in his theology toward the ahistorical side of the continuum. In addition, the shifts helped determine the issues he chose to investigate and are paradigmatic of certain movements in twentieth-century New Testament scholarship.

As I have already noted, Perrin began his career under the relatively conservative tutelage of T. W. Manson in England and Joachim Jeremias in Germany. In this early period he stood at the right side of the continuum, reflecting the position of Manson and Jeremias that the historical Jesus is of crucial importance for Christian faith. Appropriately, he advocated form criticism, a method he saw as enabling one to arrive at knowledge of the historical Jesus. He also concerned himself, appropri-

---

[26]See Norman Perrin and Dennis Duling, *The New Testament: An Introduction—Proclamation and Parenesis, Myth and History*, 2nd ed. (New York: Harcourt Brace Jovanovich, 1982 [1974]) x. Duling made no attempt to delineate the stages. See also Werner Kelber, "The Work of Norman Perrin: An Intellectual Pilgrimage," *Journal of Religion* 64 (October 1984): 452-67, where Kelber sketches Perrin's pilgrimage in terms of history, theology, and language.

[27]Perrin called his collection of articles on New Testament Christology *A Modern Pilgrimage in New Testament Christology.*

ately, with the Kingdom of God, parables, and Son of man sayings, all of which have the potential to yield knowledge about the historical Jesus.

The first major shift in Perrin's theology came as his intensive form-critical research convinced him that the main source for faith is not the historical Jesus but rather the proclamation of the early church. He refined this position by suggesting that at the level of religious belief, knowledge of the historical Jesus can, but does not necessarily, contribute to the formation of one's faith-image. His utilization of the form-critical method resulted in a shift in his theology. This shift was also related to his increasing acquaintance with Bultmann's theology.

Perrin's shift in theology was appropriate, given the results of his form-critical study of the teaching of Jesus. However, his mediating position (in the middle of the continuum) produced a certain tension in his theology that invited a more acceptable resolution. He was struggling with the basic question of whether or not Christian faith is based on history. To return to a position where it is based on history was not acceptable to him because of his form-critical conclusions about the teaching of Jesus. The only other way to reduce the tension was to move further to the left side of the continuum, a shift he eventually made.

The next shift in his work with respect to method was from form criticism to redaction criticism. There were two important reasons for this move. First, the theology that resulted from his use of form criticism—that the main source for faith is the church's proclamation—in turn prompted him to adopt redaction criticism, a method suited to uncover particular aspects of that proclamation. In other words, his new theology sought support from a new method. The second reason for the shift was form criticism's inherent tendency, at least as Perrin practiced it, to evolve into redaction criticism. In addition to the internal drive within his own work, this shift in method reflected his increasing acquaintance with the work of other redacton critics popular in the 1960s. Appropriately, his interest in redaction criticism led him to focus on the Son of man sayings in Mark and eventually to a concern for an interpretation of the whole Gospel. This shift in method was a fitting one for him to make, given the direction in which his theology was moving.

The shift to redaction criticism, in turn, produced another shift in theology. Perrin's redaction-critical findings further convinced him of the difficulty and inappropriateness of basing faith on a knowledge of the historical Jesus. As a result, his theological interests seemed to move beyond the historical Jesus, the proclamation of the church, and even the theology of the evangelists. He turned to the text of the New Testament itself as an autonomous literary object and concerned himself with hermeneutics, the dynamic interaction between the text and reader. His shift in method produced a corresponding shift in his theology. Again, given the results of his redaction-critical research, the change in theology was appropriate.

Perrin's redaction-critical work also led to an increasing appreciation for literary criticism. Again two factors encouraged his movement in this direction. First, his new and, to some degree, ahistorical theological perspective made attractive a method that enabled him to "appreciate" the text as a literary object. Second, redaction criticism, as he practiced it, shaded over into literary criticism. During this part of his career, Perrin focused on the Kingdom of God and parables, both of which are well suited for a literary approach. His final shift in method corresponded to his acquaintance with American biblical literary critics toward the end of his life. His advocacy of literary criticism was fitting because it was consistent with his most recent theological perspective.

Perrin's literary-critical turn, one that emphasized the ahistorical features of a text, did lessen the historical and theological problems associated with grounding faith in history. Yet it also created the possiblity that interpretation, when loosed from historical moorings, might become highly subjective. Because of this dilemma Perrin seemed to be moving, near the end of his life, toward a synthesis. The next shift that probably would have occured can be hypothetically constructed from suggestions in his later works, especially the programmatic essay, "Jesus and the Theology of the New Testament," and is confirmed by those who knew Perrin in his later years.

In this important essay, delivered little more than a year before his death and published only recently,[28] Perrin outlined a theology of the New Testament that would have gathered the various threads of his life's work into a unified whole. It would have creatively forged a vision of the New Testament that would drive between and beyond the two extremes of Bultmann and Jeremias. Rather than another movement along the faith and history continuum, this next shift would have been an attempt to bend the continuum into a circle that incorporated a concern for history (form criticism), theology (redaction criticism), and literature (literary criticism). Perrin had been scheduled to write the commentary on Mark in the *Hermeneia* series[29] and this synthesis would surely have found expression in his interpretation of that gospel.

Such a synthesis would, however, have culminated in a theology of the New Testament. The theological diversity of the New Testament influenced Perrin's view that academic study of the theology of the New Testament was currently in disarray. Bultmann "solved" the problem of diversity by focusing on Paul and John. Jeremias did it by emphasizing the historical Jesus. Perrin's goal was to write a theology of the New Testament that would overcome the problem by turning on the symbolic fig-

---

[28]Norman Perrin, "Jesus and the Theology of the New Testament," *Journal of Religion* 64 (October 1984): 413-31.

[29]An assignment now given to Perrin's student, John R. Donahue.

ure of Jesus as the unifying factor and the one constant in all the different theological systems in the New Testament. This symbolic figure is the faith-image of Christ rather than the historical Jesus. He planned to interpret the diverse traditions of the New Testament in terms of how the Jesus figure functioned within these various traditions.

The strength of such a theology would have been Perrin's expertise in the synoptics and his methodological flexibility; its weakness would have revealed his lack of depth in Pauline and Johannine studies. Despite this weakness, Perrin's developing theology could, potentially, have pointed the way toward an integrated approach to biblical studies; it could also have established him as the leading New Testament scholar in America.

•PART I•

THE DEVELOPMENT OF AN EXEGETICAL METHODOLOGY

THE CONTINENTAL HERITAGE: HISTORICAL CRITICISM

• From Form Criticism to Redaction Criticism. •

By the turn of the century, most scholars had accepted the view that the two sources for Matthew and Luke were Mark and *Quelle* (usually designated "Q"), a term that refers to sayings material contained in Matthew and Luke but not in Mark. An important motivation, on the part of many scholars, for determining the original sources of the gospels was the presupposition that success would mean the possibility of writing a history of the earthly Jesus. Such optimism was blunted even as the source conclusions were being reached. Most important in this regard was William Wrede's 1901 work on the "Messianic Secret" motif in Mark.[1] Wrede argued that Mark, even though it is thought to be the oldest gospel and closest to the events of Jesus' life, is not a straightforward, historically trustworthy account of the life of Jesus. On the contrary, Mark's picture of Jesus was influenced by theological concerns. Determining the earliest sources (Mark and Q) did not provide the materials to construct a life of Jesus, and so a desire to get behind these sources necessitated a more sophisticated approach to gospel study, a need met by form criticism.

Form criticism (in German, *Formgeschichte*) is a method of studying and analyzing materials which have been passed on orally for some period of time. This approach was of utmost importance to Life of Jesus researchers because it helped to determine what material in the gospels reflected the creative activity of the early church and what material originated with the historical Jesus.

Rudolf Bultmann, the most influential of the early form critics, provided in *The History of the Synoptic Tradition*[2] the first full-scale form-criti-

---

[1]Wilhelm Wrede, *The Messianic Secret,* trans. J. C. G. Greig (Cambridge: Clarke, 1971 [1901]).

[2]Rudolf Bultmann, *The History of the Synoptic Tradition,* rev. ed., trans. John Marsh (New York: Harper and Row, 1963 [1921]).

cal treatment of the entire synoptic tradition. Bultmann's work led him to rather skeptical conclusions concerning the authenticity of much of the material and, therefore, to skepticism about the possibility of discovering much about the historical Jesus.

Although Bultmann has been the most influential scholar to use form criticism, the method has been practiced by scholars who arrive at very different conclusions concerning the historical reliability of the synoptic tradition. Perhaps the most significant conservative use of form criticism was that of Joachim Jeremias. Jeremias accepted form criticism as a valuable research tool, but was not satisfied with its negative results. He argued that form criticism was valuable in enabling one to work back from the Hellenistic layer of tradition to the Palestinian-Aramaic level. Jeremias's *New Testament Theology: The Proclamation of Jesus*[3] was the best presentation of his method and main conclusions. Published in 1971, it was the *summa* of Jeremias's research over the years and was a compendium of the work reflected in earlier books.

Jeremias is important in a consideration of the history and deveopment of form criticism because he represents a perspective different from that of a generation of scholars so heavily influenced by Bultmann. While Bultmann was a master of Greek and the Hellenistic world, Jeremias' forte was his interest and expertise in the Aramaic/Jewish background of the New Testament, an interest that stemmed from his boyhood years in Palestine and his studies with Aramaic scholar Gustav Dalman. Again and again Jeremias dug back to a primitive Palestinian tradition by applying linguistic and stylistic criteria to the synoptic tradition of the sayings of Jesus. In addition, Jeremias's respect for the tradition led him to affirm that it was the inauthenticity, not authenticity, of the sayings attributed to Jesus that must be demonstrated.[4] Bultmann assumed that the burden of proof was on the claim to authenticity.

In recounting the history of form criticism, Edgar V. McKnight[5] found it helpful to identify two movements in the twentieth century form-critical quest for the historical Jesus. The conservative movement, which included scholars like Jeremias, Vincent Taylor, and T. W. Manson, Perrin's teacher, continued the quest for the historical Jesus with some confidence. Bultmann stood at the fountainhead of the skeptical movement that denied the possibility of a comprehensive life of Jesus, and concentrated on the creative contributions of the church to the synoptic tradition.

---

[3]Joachim Jeremias, *New Testament Theology: The Proclamation of Jesus,* trans. John Bowden (New York: Charles Scribner's Sons, 1971).

[4]Ibid., 37. See also Jeremias, *The Prayers of Jesus,* trans. John Bowden et al., second series 6 of Studies in Biblical Theology (Naperville IL: Alec R. Allenson, 1967) 108.

[5]Edgar V. McKnight, *What is Form Criticism?* Guides to Biblical Scholarship, ed. Dan O. Via, Jr. (Philadelphia: Fortress Press, 1969) 57.

The "new quest" of the historical Jesus, which included some of Bultmann's students,—including Ernst Käsemann, Ernst Fuchs, and Günther Bornkamm—accepted Bultmann's basic orientation toward the synoptic tradition and recognized the impossibility of writing a comprehensive biography of Jesus. The modification of Bultmann's historical work by the new questers came in their argument that additional material could be attributed to the person and especially to the teaching of Jesus.

Redaction criticism (in German, *Redaktionsgeschichte)* is a method of studying an author's work to determine how and why that author chose and modified materials available in the tradition. Redaction criticism can be viewed as a natural extenson of form criticism in that the author stood at the final stage of the development of a tradition. From this perspective, redaction criticism can be important in Life of Jesus research because it enables one to identify elements in the tradition that are to be attributed to the evangelists and not to the historical Jesus.[6] Redaction criticism came to fruition in the 1950s and 1960s in the work of Bornkamm on Matthew, Hans Conzelmann on Luke, and Willi Marxsen on Mark.

With respect to method in Life of Jesus and synoptic research, Perrin's work developed along the general lines just outlined. He assumed, but never discussed at any length, the source-critical concluson that the four basic sources of the synoptic gospels are Mark, Q, M, and L.[7] He appropriated and entered fully into the theoretical discussion of form criticism, then redaction criticism, and later literary criticism. While his work developed in stages that can be labeled form criticism, readaction criticism, and literary criticism, it must be emphasized that these were not clearly defined stages because each one evolved gradually into the next one.

Nowhere in his first book or the three articles which preceded it did Perrin give explicit attention to the question of method in the interpretation of the New Testament. While he did not explicitly acknowledge it, in *Kingdom of God* he assumed the results of form-critical work on the synoptics. He utilized only sayings that various form critics have attributed to the historical Jesus, such as the Lord's Prayer, apocalyptic Son of man sayings and Beatitudes.

Although Perrin did not give explicit attention to any method per se, he did, in his first published article, review favorably how three of Bultmann's students (Käsemann, Bornkamm, and Fuchs) found more authentic material in the synoptics than did their teacher.[8] Perrin's inclination

---

[6]Life of Jesus research, however, did not seem to be a major concern for many redaction critics.

[7]See, for example, Norman Perrin, *Rediscovering the Teaching of Jesus* (New York: Harper and Row 1967) 53.

[8]Norman Perrin and William R. Farmer, "The Kerygmatic Theology and the Question of the Historical Jesus," *Religion in Life* 29 (Winter 1959-1960): 97.

toward the results of Bultmann's students rather than toward those of their teacher, reflected the influence of his conservative British and German heritage. Perrin dedicated his first book, *Kingdom of God,*

> To those two great New Testament scholars with whom it has been the author's privilege to study: T. W. Manson of Manchester and J. Jeremias of Göttingen.[9]

Jeremias was Perrin's *Doktorvater* in Germany. He advised Perrin in the writing of his doctoral dissertation, later revised and published as *Kingdom of God.* Manson, Jeremias, and Taylor, another British form critic with whose work Perrin was familiar, all reflected this same conservative confidence in the synoptic tradition exhibited by Perrin at the beginning of his work.

Within a few years of the publication of *Kingdom of God,* Perrin had entered fully into the discussion of the theory and technique of form criticism. Although he treated the subject of method in several articles, his most extended and important discussion was found in chapter 1 of *Rediscovering,* where he referred to form criticism as "the single most important development in the history of the discussion of our problem."[10] He went on to provide a systematic presentation of the form-critical method as he used it in that book.[11]

The most crucial part of Perrin's discussion of method was his sharpening of three important criteria that must be applied to the saying of Jesus to determine if those sayings are authentic. The "fundamental criterion for authenticity" was termed the "criterion of dissimilarity." In Perrin's formulation, "the earliest form of a saying we can reach may be regarded as authentic if it can be shown to be dissimilar to characteristic emphases both of ancient Judaism and of the early church." Perrin assumed that, given the nature of the synoptic tradition, the burden of proof was on those who would claim a saying to be authentic.[12] This assumption explained the first part of the formulation—that to claim authenticity, one must show that a saying came neither from the church nor from ancient Judaism. His position here was significantly different from that of Je-

---

[9]Norman Perrin, *The Kingdom of God in the Teaching of Jesus* (Philadelphia: Westminster Press, 1963) 1.

[10]Perrin, *Rediscovering,* 218.

[11]Actually, the seeds that grew into *Rediscovering* can be found in Perrin's 1962 lecture series entitled "The Teaching of Jesus." Although it was aimed at the laity, Perrin felt that the lecture series helped him think through and develop the general choice of topic and method of treatment. David Abernathy, Perrin's friend and student at Emory, helped him organize the material and edit the tapes. Abernathy later updated the work and published it as *Understanding the Teaching of Jesus* (New York: Seabury Press, 1983).

[12]Perrin, *Rediscovering,* 39.

iterion of dissimilarity."[18] Edgar V. McKnight, in his helpful introduc-
on to form criticism, reported that the criterion of coherence or consis-
ncy was suggested by C. E. Carlston in 1962 to compensate for the radical
nsequences of relying solely on the criterion of dissimilarity.[19] Perrin,
owever, found traces of the use of this criterion in Bultmann's *History of
e Synoptic Tradition* and *Jesus and the Word*.[20] Bultmann, according to Per-
n, grouped together sayings that showed similar characteristics and was
ot concerned if some of these sayings were of doubtful authenticity on
her grounds.

> What he does is to use any saying from the earliest stratum of the tradition
> which expresses something he has previously determined to be character-
> istic of the teaching of Jesus. This is in practice the criterion we have sought
> to formulate in principle.[21]

rrin also attributed Jeremias with using this principle in his book, *Un-
own Sayings of Jesus*.[22] Here Jeremias identified twenty-one sayings as
ving as high a claim to authenticity as any synoptic saying because they
e "perfectly compatible with" *(sich einfügen)* the genuine sayings.[23] The
ly essential difference between the use of this criterion by Jeremias and
rrin was that Jeremias applied it to noncanonical traditions while Per-
n, like Bultmann, proposed to use it on the synoptic tradition.[24]

The third basic criterion Perrin identified was what he called "multi-
e attestation," a term borrowed from Harvey K. McArthur,[25] and de-
ed as "a proposal to accept as authentic material which is attested in
, or most, of the sources which can be discerned behind the synoptic
spels."[26] Perrin traced the use of this criterion to English scholars and
inted out that T. W. Manson had made particular use of it.[27] For Man-

---

[18]Ibid.

[19]McKnight, *What is Form Criticism?*, 66.

[20]Rudolf Bultmann, *Jesus and the Word*, trans. Louise P. Smith and Erminie H.
ntero (New York: Charles Scribner's Sons, 1934 [1926]).

[21]Perrin, *Rediscovering*, 44.

[22]Joachim Jeremias, *Unknown Sayings of Jesus*, trans. R. H. Fuller (London: SPCK,
7 [1951]).

[23]Ibid., 30; see Perrin, *Rediscovering*, 45.

[24]Perrin, *Rediscovering*, 45.

[25]Harvey K. McArthur, "Basic Issues, A Survey of Recent Gospel Research,"
rpretation 18 (January 1964): 39-55.

[26]Perrin, *Rediscovering*, 45.

[27]See, for example, T. W. Manson, *The Teachings of Jesus: Studies of Its Form and
tent*, 2nd. ed. (Cambridge: Cambridge University Press, 1955 [1935]); and *The
ings of Jesus* (London: SCM Press, 1949 [1937]).

remias, who said it was the inauthenticity, not the a
sayings of Jesus that must be demonstrated.[13] Perrin
rion of dissimilarity was first used by Bultmann who a
ables.[14] He also credited Jeremias with utilizing such a
his work on the use of *abba* and on the formula, "Amen,
Perrin was especialy indebted to Ernst Käsemann[15] in
mulation of this criterion and noted its use by Conzel

Numerous scholars have criticized the criterion
cause it does not allow as authentic sayings that Jesus
if such utterances are similar to the early church or Jud
Helmut Koester, in his perceptive evaluation of *Redisco*
criterion that

> it does not always guide us in our search for the relat
> teaching to his Jewish tradition and environment, nor
> lead us into the problems of nascent Christianity in its
> and confirm a continuity of its own beliefs with Jesus an
> works.[16]

This criterion, then, provides only an irreducible minim
the historical Jesus, but it does not admit material wl
to Jesus' environment of Judaism or to the early chur
sus. Perrin himself recognized this limitation.

> Of course, it is limited in scope—by definition it will e
> in which Jesus may have been at one with Judaism or t
> one with him. But the brutal fact of the matter is that v
> There simply is no other starting-point that takes ser
> radical view of the nature of the sources which the resul
> research are forcing upon us.[17]

In Perrin's program, the criterion of dissimilarity
material that could then serve as a foundation on w
lizing a second criterion, coherence. As he explained
earliest strata of the tradition may be accepted as a
shown to cohere with material established as authe

---

[13]Jeremias, *New Testament Theology*, 37.

[14]Bultmann, *History of the Synoptic Tradition*, 205.

[15]Ernst Käsemann, "The Problem of the Historical Jesus
tament Themes, trans. W. J. Montague, Studies in Biblical
SCM Press, 1964 [1960]).

[16]Helmut Koester, "The Historical Jesus: Some Comn
Norman Perrin's *Rediscovering the Teachings of Jesus*," in H
tology and a Modern Pilgrimage: A Discussion with Norman
Scholar's Press, 1971) 124.

[17]Perrin, *Rediscovering*, 43.

son, when a saying was found in both Mark and Q, it was considered authentic. Since Perrin did not have the same respect for the historical value of the sources, he had reservations about using this method to isolate the very words of Jesus. Multiple attestation was helpful, he said, in

> establishing the authenticity of motifs from the ministry of Jesus, although rarely that of specific sayings. . . . We may say that a motif which can be detected in a multiplicity of strands of tradition and in various forms (pronouncement stories, parables, sayings, etc.) will have a high claim to authenticity, always provided that it is not characteristic of an activity, interest or emphasis of the earliest Church.[28]

Finally, Perrin summarized the way in which he proposed to blend these three criteria.

> Our procedure will be to attempt to arrive at elements in the tradition which have a high claim to authenticity and then to move out from there, going from the specific to the general rather than vice versa. We shall therefore have only limited occasion to use the criterion of multiple attestation, preferring to work upon the basis of the establishment of the history of the tradition and the criteria of dissimilarity and coherence.[29]

Perrin advanced the work of form criticism by his careful sharpening of the criteria of authenticity. With each of the three criteria, he attempted to trace its use back to earlier scholars, thereby indicating that he was not the first to use it. Neither was he the first to delineate criteria for authenticity in a straightforward fashion. McArthur, in his 1964 article, identified four criteria: multiple attestation, tendencies of the developing tradition discounted, attestation by multiple forms, and elimination of all material which may be derived either from Judaism or from primitive Christianity.[30] At the same time that Perrin was developing his three criteria, Reginald H. Fuller was independently developing the same three criteria, which he called distinctiveness, cross-section method, and consistency.[31] Perrin's terminology caught on and since the publication of *Rediscovering*, dissimilarity, coherence, and multiple attestation have usually been regarded in introductory textbooks as the basic criteria that form critics use to determine authenticity.

Thus far the discussion has concentrated on Perrin's formulation of the criteria of authenticity because this formulation was fundamental to

---

[28]Perrin, *Rediscovering*, 46.

[29]Ibid., 47.

[30]McArthur, "Basic Issues," 39-55.

[31]Reginald H. Fuller, *A Critical Introduction to the New Testament* (Naperville IL: Alec R. Allenson, 1966) 94-98. Fuller also included a fourth criterion, linguistic and environmental tests, a criterion Perrin subsumed under the task of writing the history of a particular saying.

his analysis of the synoptic gospels, and the terminology he suggested was his most important contribution to the development of form-critical theory and practice. However, a complete understanding of his program of form criticism must include his belief about the nature of the synoptic gospels. Crucial here was his view that

> the early Church made no attempt to distinguish between the words the earthly Jesus had spoken and those spoken by the risen Lord through a prophet in the community. . . . The early Church absolutely and completely identified the risen Lord of her experience with the earthly Jesus of Nazareth and created for her purposes, which she conceived to be his, the literary form of the gospel, in which words and deeds ascribed in his consciousness to both the earthly Jesus and risen Lord were set down in terms of the former.[32]

This understanding was so basic for him that he stated it over and over in various ways.[33] Because of this feature of the synoptic materials, Perrin found it necessary to write a history of the tradition before applying the criteria of authenticity.

In his concern to write a history of the tradition, Perrin reflected the early form-critical emphasis of Martin Dibelius and Bultmann, both of whom were interested in the "setting in life" *(Sitz im Leben)* of each unit of the tradition. To help in writing the history of a particular saying, Perrin employed the linguistic features (such as Aramaisms) that had been used so effectively by Jeremias. Jeremias sought to set the sayings against an Aramaic background in order to get behind the Hellenistic layer of tradition. It is important to realize that reaching the Aramaic layer does not mean that one has reached "the very words of Jesus." It is possible that one may have reached only the Aramaic-speaking church. At this point, Perrin applied the criterion of dissimilarity.[34]

Because it was of crucial import for Perrin's program that this characteristic of the material be admitted, he devoted a considerable amount of space in the first chapter of *Rediscovering* to refuting certain arguments against it. From Roman Catholic and conservative Protestant scholarship arguments had been made against notions of the creative power of the early church and the lack of interest in history. Such arguments usually centered around insistence that eyewitnesses kept the tradition from changing or that Jesus like later rabbis, taught his disciples by using memory texts, and therefore preserved the tradition. Perrin took up these points one by one.

---

[32]Perrin, *Rediscovering*, 15.

[33]For example, ibid., 16, 26, 27, 31, 219.

[34]Ibid., 37.

His essential answer to this criticism from the right was that conservative scholars like Birger Gerhardsson[35] had not based their theories on careful exegetical work that explained the observable phenomena in the texts. "We must insist that the crux of the matter is to explain the phenomena present in the texts."[36] Form criticism, Perrin was convinced, provided this explanation.

As I pointed out earlier, form critics often had very different views concerning the historical reliability of the synoptic gospels. Consequently, they arrived at very different conclusions about what is authentic in the gospel material. Conservative form criticism can be seen in the work of Jeremias, Manson, and Taylor, while a more radical approach was taken by Bultmann. For several reasons Perrin is clearly to be identified with the skeptical approach of Bultmann rather than the conservative approach of Jeremias, Manson, and Taylor. First, contrary to Jeremias, he argued that the burden of proof was on the claim to authenticity rather than the claim to inauthenticity. Second, unlike Manson, he proposed to use the criterion of multiple attestation only in a limited way, preferring instead to use the more stringent criteria of dissimilarity and coherence. Finally, he proposed to reconstruct the history of the tradition of a particular saying before applying the criterion of dissimilarity. Since Perrin, unlike Gerhardsson, accentuated the creative power of the early church and its lack of interest in history, sayings did not easily survive his reconstructions.

Although *Rediscovering* reflected an essentially Bultmannian position with respect to method, Perrin's careful delineation of criteria of authenticity pointed to a difference in emphasis between himself and Bultmann. He was more interested than Bultmann in Life of Jesus research. Insofar as he had this interest in the historical Jesus, Perrin can be identified with the "new quest," which was also interested in showing that more than Bultmann would admit could be discovered about Jesus.[37]

In the 1960s Perrin became increasingly aware of the significance of redaction criticism, an approach to studying the synoptic gospels that had arisen in the 1950s and had become popular in the 1960s. *Rediscovering* appeared in 1967, an attempt at Life of Jesus research using form criticism. One year before it was published, Perrin wrote an article celebrating the rise of redaction criticism. The article was entitled "The *Wredestrasse* Becomes the *Hauptstrasse*" ("The Wrede-road Becomes the Chief-road"); the first part of the title was an allusion to a statement made by Perrin's teacher, Manson. In his evaluation of the work of Wrede, Manson had

---

[35]See Gerhardsson's *Memory and Manuscript* (Lund: C. W. K. Gleerup, 1964 [1961]).

[36]Perrin, *Rediscovering*, 32.

[37]On Perrin's interest in Life of Jesus research, see ibid., 11.

written, "The further we travel along the *Wredestrasse,* the clearer it becomes that it is the road to nowhere."[38] Perrin viewed Wrede's work as inaugurating redaction criticism of the gospels. After surveying some of the important redaction-critical literature on the synoptic gospels, he concluded, against his old teacher, that "The *Wredestrasse* has become the *Hauptstrasse,* and it is leading us to new and exciting country."[39]

Almost immediately after the form-critical *Rediscovering* was published, Perrin began to approach the Gospel of Mark using redaction criticism. In an article he analyzed Mark's "creative" use of the Son of man traditions.[40] He continued successfully to interpret Mark by using redaction criticism and became a strong advocate and able practitioner of the method. One interpreter went so far as to call him "North America's best known exponent of redaction criticism."[41] That Perrin was highly regarded as a redaction critic was demonstrated when he was chosen to write the exposition of this form of criticism in the Guides to Biblical Scholarship series. In this book, *What is Redaction Criticism?*, he wrote that New Testament redaction criticism was

> concerned with studying the theological motivation of an author as this is revealed in the collection, arrangement, editing, and modification of traditional material, and in the composition of new material or the creation of new forms within the traditions of early Christianity.

Perrin preferred to translate *Redaktionsgeschichte* (literally redaction history) as redaction criticism in order to keep the terminology consistent with the terms literary or source criticism and form criticism. Although he used here the designation redaction criticism, he went on to say that this method could also be termed "composition criticism."[42] When he wrote this book, he used redaction criticism as an umbrella term to include redaction of previous units of tradition and composition of new material.

> It refers to the whole range of creative activities which we can detect in a

---

[38]T. W. Manson, "The Life of Jesus: Some Tendencies in Present-Day Research," in W. D. Davies and David Daube, eds., *The Background of the New Testament and Its Eschatology* (Cambridge: Cambridge University Press, 1964 [1956]) 216.

[39]Norman Perrin, "The *Wredestrasse* Becomes the *Hauptstrasse:* Reflections on the Reprinting of the Dodd *Festschrift," Journal of Religion* 46 (April 1966): 297-98.

[40]Norman Perrin, "The Creative Use of the Son of Man Tradition by Mark," *Union Seminary Quarterly Review* 23 (1967-1968): 237-65.

[41]Peter Richardson, "Review of *What is Redaction Criticism?" Canadian Journal of Theology* 16 (1970): 106.

[42]Norman Perrin, *What Is Redaction Criticism?* Guides to Biblical Scholarship, ed. Dan O. Via, Jr. (Philadelphia: Fortress Press, 1969) 1.

evangelist, an author, a transmitter of tradition, and in which and by means of which we learn something of that author's, evangelist's, transmitter's theology.[43]

At the same time Perrin suggested that the discipline may develop to the extent that redaction criticism may have to be distinguished from composition criticism,[44] although he never made this specific distinction.

One of the characteristics of Perrin as a redaction critic was that, as an able practitioner of form criticism, he was able to show the close relationship between form and redaction criticism. He called the two approaches the "first and second stages of a unified discipline."[45] He viewed William Wrede's work on the Messianic Secret motif in Mark as creating a demand for the discipline of form criticism and preparing the way for redaction criticism. Wrede's work called for form criticism because it emphasized the necessity of writing a history of the tradition before the work of the evangelist could be isolated. Wrede's work prepared the way for redaction criticism by pointing out that the secrecy motif developed because of dogmatic ideas at work in the tradition. Redaction criticism later built on Wrede's insight by defining more particularly Mark's contribution to the development.[46]

Under the continuing impact of form criticism and the increasing use of redaction criticism, Perrin became more skeptical of the possiblity of obtaining much knowledge of the historical Jesus from a study of the synoptic gospels.

> That redaction criticism makes Life of Jesus research very much more difficult is, of course, immediately obvious. With the recognition that so very much of the material in the Gospels must be ascribed to the theological motivation of the evangelist or of an editor of the tradition, or of a prophet or preacher in the early church, we must come to recognize that the words of R. H. Lightfoot were fully and absolutely justified: the Gospels do indeed yield us "only the whisper of Jesus' voice."[47]

Perrin pointed out that in earlier Life of Jesus research (and in some more recent work like Morna D. Hooker's *The Son of Man in Mark*)[48] the burden of proof for a Jesus saying was on the claim of inauthenticity. Now he contended that the burden was on the claim to authenticity and the dif-

---

[43]Ibid., 66.

[44]Ibid., 67.

[45]Ibid., 2.

[46]Ibid., 12-13.

[47]Ibid., 69.

[48]Morna D. Hooker, *The Son of Man in Mark: A Study of the Background of the Term "Son of Man" and Its Use in St. Mark's Gospel* (Montreal: McGill University Press, 1967).

ficulties of establishing that claim become "very great—very great indeed, but not impossible."[49]

Perrin's best systematic presentation of that knowledge, in light of form and redaction criticism, is found in the final chapter of his *Introduction*.[50] He began this presentation by emphasizing that in the Jesus tradition past reminiscence, present experience, and future expectation by the Christians became fused in the story of the life and teaching of the earthly Jesus. Given this situation, the task of the Life of Jesus researcher was to disentangle the present experience and future expectation from the actual reminiscence.

At the time of the publication of *Redaction Criticism*, Perrin's reflection on method was limited to redaction criticism understood in the narrow sense of redaction of previous material and composition of new material. By the early 1970s, he began to expand his understanding of method into a multifaceted approach. This progression was a natural development of Perrin's view, noted earlier, that redaction criticism referred to the "whole range of creative activities which we can detect in an evangelist, an author, a transmitter of tradition."[51] That sentence, written in 1969, suggests there is more to the activity of the gospel writers than their redaction and composition. However, it was not until the early 1970s when Perrin came under the influence of American literary criticism, that he began to reflect more specifically on this "whole range of creative activities."

• The Problem of the Historical Jesus. •

Perrin's pilgrimage from form criticism to redaction criticism and finally to literary criticism can be understood as a result of an inherent methodological thrust and scholarly influences. There was also a basic theological issue that provided an essential motivation for such a movement—the relationship between faith and history. The issue was, specifically, the significance of the historical Jesus for Christian faith—or, as Patrick Henry put it, "How much history is enough?"[52]

The question of the significance of the historical Jesus for faith became an important issue as modern biblical scholarship gained the opportunity and the tools to do historical research. The Renaissance, with its creative impulse toward exploration to the past and present world, contributed to the rise of a historical approach to the Bible, especially in the area of textual criticism. W. G. Kümmel, in his history of New Testament scholar-

[49]Perrin, *Redaction Criticism*, 70.

[50]Norman Perrin, *The New Testament: An Introduction—Proclamation and Parenesis, Myth and History* (New York: Harcourt Brace Jovanovich, 1974) 277-303.

[51]Perrin, *Redaction Criticism*, 66.

[52]Patrick Henry, *New Directions in New Testament Study* (Philadelphia: Westminster Press, 1979) 120.

ship to 1930, viewed modern, scientific research on the Bible as stemming in part from the Protestant Reformation which encouraged biblical exegesis that was no longer hampered by the authoritative teaching of the Roman Catholic church. The Enlightenment spirit of inquiry at the bar of reason, a spirit freed from dogmatic concerns imposed from an outside orthodoxy and finding powerful expression in eighteenth century English deism, helped to provide the rationalistic tools for a historical approach.[53]

Hermann S. Reimarus (1694-1768) is often viewed as beginning the scholarly quest for the historical Jesus, the Jesus as he actually was. He suggested that the disciples were all frauds and that the Christ who appears in the gospels is a product of deceptive disciples and is not consistent with the historical Jesus. Reimarus's radical distinction between the historical Jesus and the report of the evangelists about him became one of the major issues in the subsequent debate. It was in the nineteenth century, though, that historical study of the New Testament bore the most significant fruit and began to define more particularly the issue of the significance of the historical Jesus for faith. The first major contribution to the discussion came from David F. Strauss.

Strauss's *The Life of Jesus Critically Examined*,[54] which appeared in its first edition in 1835, was important because it refuted previous approaches and anticipated subsequent studies in the reconstruction and meaning of the historical Jesus. Strauss denied the legitimacy of the then-current supernaturalistic construction of the Life of Jesus by orthodoxy as well as the rationalistic constructions that provided naturalistic explanations for Jesus' life. His approach was to explain the supernatural in the gospels as myth. That the gospels were essentially mythological did not seem to disturb Strauss, who, although he did not devote any attention to it directly, implied that the basis of faith was transhistorical truth. He did make it clear that the basis of faith was not anything historical. Strauss later, in the context of a critique of Schleiermacher's *Life of Jesus*,[55] provided a more contructive suggestion about the basis of Christian faith by separating the "Jesus of history" from "the Christ of faith." The approach he began to take in this later work found cogent expression in the work of Martin Kähler, discussed later in this chapter.

---

[53]Werner G. Kümmel, *The New Testament: The History of the Investigation of Its Problems*, 2nd ed., trans. S. McLean Gilmour and Howard C. Kee (Nashville: Abingdon Press, 1972 [1958]) 20ff., 51ff.

[54]David F. Strauss, *The Life of Jesus, Critically Examined*, 4th ed., ed. Peter C. Hodgson, trans. George Eliot (Philadelphia: Fortress Press, 1972).

[55]See David F. Strauss, *The Christ of Faith and the Jesus of History: A Critique of Schleiermacher's "Life of Jesus,"* trans. Leander E. Keck (Philadelphia: Fortress Press, 1977 [1865]).

The negative conclusions of Strauss, however, served to encourage others to attempt a more positive answer to the question of the significance of the historical Jesus. The result, which dominated much nineteenth-century scholarship, has often been referred to as the quest for the historical Jesus. The lives of Jesus that resulted from this quest came from the pens of scholars who enthusiastically and confidently attempted to push back through the strange, apocalyptic ideas of the gospels. These lives of Jesus were usually molded in the liberal tradition and painted a Jesus who exhibited the timeless message of the fatherhood of God, the brotherhood of men, and the ethic of love. From a scholarly perspective, the problem with these lives of Jesus was that they more often than not reflected the liberal (or perhaps idealist, rationalist, socialist, or romanticist) view of the writer rather than the actual historical Jesus.

What is important for the purposes of this study, however, is that these quests for the historical Jesus were generally predicated on two important assumptions. First, the questers assumed that the historical Jesus could be discovered if the sources were properly evaluated. The establishment of the priority of Mark as a source for Matthew and Luke, a source-critical suggestion that was introduced in 1835 and gained increasing popularity through the nineteenth century, gave impetus to the quest because scholars had confidence in the historical reliability of the oldest sources.

A second and, for the purposes of this chapter, more important assumption, was that the historical Jesus was significant for faith and therefore should be discovered. This assumption was the cornerstone of the liberal quest. Liberal theology, which gained increasing influence in the second half of the nineteenth century, emphasized that the ethical nature of the Christian life was grounded in the historical revelation in Jesus. Albrecht Ritschl is often called the father of liberal theology. One of the best examples of liberal theology is the series of lectures delivered by Adolf von Harnack in 1899-1900 and published in English as *What is Christianity?*[56] Building on the work of Ritschl, Harnack maintained that one finds the essence of the Christian faith in the person and especially the teaching of Jesus. That teaching, located in the synoptic gospels, was understood in the liberal tradition of the loving Father and the infinite value of the human soul.

Several important developments at the end of the nineteenth century and the beginning of the twentieth contributed to the end of the quest of the historical Jesus. One was the breakdown of the assumption that the supposed earliest source, Mark, was a historically reliable document. Another development contributing to the end of the quest was the recognition that apocalyptic eschatology was an essential element in Jesus'

---

[56]Adolf von Harnack, *What Is Christianity?* 3rd ed., trans. Thomas Bailey Saunders (New York: G. P. Putnam's Sons, 1912).

preaching. This recognition was a severe blow, especially to the liberal quest. The problem was how a Jesus who incorrectly preached that the end of the world was imminent could be significant for faith. Albert Schweitzer's *The Quest of the Historical Jesus*[57] can, in retrospect, be viewed as a final epitaph to the liberal quest. In summarizing the quest up to 1901, Schweitzer demonstrated how the old questers failed to reach the historical Jesus because they read their own image of Jesus into the sources.

The most important blow to the quest was the notion that it was not necessary because the historical Jesus was not significant for faith. Strauss had made such as suggestion in his acknowledgment that the Christian faith did not depend on the results of his critical investigation into the gospels. But the first, important attempt to delineate carefully the various aspects of the issue from an acknowledged theological angle was Martin Kähler's book, *The So-called Historical Jesus and the Historic Biblical Christ.*[58]

Kähler made a sharp attack on Life of Jesus research by denying the significance of the nineteenth-century quests, which he called a "blind alley."[59] He argued that the gospels were not intended to be biographical memoirs of Jesus, and furthermore, that whatever historical knowledge was obtained was provisional and could be disputed by subsequent research. The object of faith was the transhistorical Christ and not the Jesus of historical reconstruction. Specifically, he drew a distinction between the historical Jesus *(der historische Jesus)* who was known through scientific research and the historic, preached Christ *(der geschichtliche Christus)* who was significant for faith.

Two features of Kähler's work eventually proved to be important contributions to the discussion. First is Kähler's distincton between *historische* and *geschichtliche,* two adjectives often translated into English, respectively, as "historical" and "historic."[60] The historical has to do with the actual events of history. The historic has to do with the significance of events for human beings. Much later debate on the issue of the significance of the historical Jesus can be framed around the question of how far the difference and distinction between the historical Jesus and the historic Christ should be pressed. A second contribution by Kähler is his insistence that it is the historic Christ, the preached Christ, and not the historical Jesus that is the object of faith.

---

[57]Albert Schweitzer, *The Quest of the Historical Jesus: A Critical Study of Its Progress from Reimarus to Wrede,* trans. W. Montgomery (New York: Macmillan, 1968 [1906]).

[58]Martin Kähler, *The So-Called Historical Jesus and the Historic Biblical Christ,* trans. and ed. Carl E. Braaten (Philadelphia: Fortress Press, 1964 [1896]).

[59]Ibid., 46.

[60]Kähler was not always consistent in his use of these terms, as Braaten pointed out in the introduction to his translation of Kähler's book (20). Yet Kähler certainly helped to create the distinction now accepted in the discussion.

The historical criticism of the quest by Schweitzer, Wrede, and others and the theological criticism by Kähler discouraged attempts to discover the historical Jesus. It was however, the form critics—and especially Rudolf Bultmann—who dealt the most devastating blow to the quest. Bultmann, the premier form critic, took positions on both the critical possibility and the theological necessity of discovering the historical Jesus. His skeptical conclusion with regard to the former has already been discussed. With regard to the latter, his contribution to the discussion, developed in several articles and books,[61] deeply influenced subsequent scholars, including Perrin.

Bultmann approached the issue of the significance of the historical Jesus from a particular philosophical perspective. Behind Bultmann stood the existentialist philosopher Martin Heidegger. Borrowing from Heidegger, Bultmann employed the notions of inauthentic and authentic existence. Inauthentic existence is losing oneself in one's surroudings and is characterized by fear and anxiety. To use biblical terms, inauthentic existence is standing outside faith and corresponds to the notions of sin, fear, flesh, and death. Authentic existence is standing in faith and corresponds to the new life of salvation and giving oneself to God. To Bultmann, the teaching of the New Testament was expressed in mythological language such as sin, demons, atonement, and heaven. Existentialist categories were his way of bridging the gap between these mythological notions and modernity or, to use the usual term, they were his way of "demythologizing" the New Testament.

Bultmann drew a distinction between the Proclaimer (Kähler's historical Jesus) and the Proclaimed (Kähler's historic Christ). The object of faith is the Proclaimed. The challenge of Christ comes in the peaching, in the kerygma. Bultmann, then, was diametrically opposed to those who held that the basis for Christian faith is in any sense historical. Because he believed the historical Jesus is not significant for faith, he was not disturbed by his form-critical findings that the sources can assure us only *that* Jesus lived and died. To base faith on the historical is to seek objective verification for faith in historically proven facts. Such seeking is contrary not only to the Reformation tradition in which Bultmann stood, but also to the nature of faith itself, which dictates that one find security in "the unseen beyond, in God."[62]

---

[61]See, for example, Rudolf Bultmann, *Jesus and the Word;* "New Testament and Mythology" (1941) trans. R. H. Fuller, in *Kerygma and Myth* (New York: Harper and Row, 1961); "The Primitive Christian Kerygma and the Historical Jesus" (1962) in *The Historical Jesus and the Kerygmatic Christ: Essays in the New Quest of the Historical Jesus,* trans. Carl E. Braaten and Roy A. Harrisville (New York: Abingdon Press, 1964) 15-42; *Faith and Understanding,* 6th ed., trans. Louise Pettibone Smith (London: SCM Press, 1969); and *Jesus Christ and Mythology* (New York: Charles Scribner's Sons, 1958).

[62]Bultmann, *Jesus Christ and Mythology,* 40.

This view of the nature of faith became the context for the often-quoted statement by Bultmann that *"The message of Jesus* is a presupposition for the theology of the New Testament rather than a part of that theology itself."[63] The theology of the New Testament, for him, was taken largely from John and Paul and, like John and Paul, Bultmann focused on the Christ of the kerygma and not the historical Jesus.

Bultmann represented a position concerning the significance of the historical Jesus that was almost opposite to that of the nineteenth-century quest. However, some scholars have taken an even more radical stance than he. They include theologian Fritz Buri,[64] theologian Schubert Ogden,[65] and philosopher Karl Jaspers.[66] All three generally insisted that Bultmann's program, if consistently followed, leads to the demythologizing of the act of God itself and the abandonment of a faith that is necessarily Christian. Their position, while perhaps a consistent application of Bultmann's theology, has not achieved as much influence as the position of Bultmann.

Although Bultmann's kerygmatic interpretation had enormous impact on the subsequent discussion, it should not be thought that it swept all scholars into its fold. Those scholars who can be viewed as holding to the possibility, albeit in a modified form, of continuing the nineteenth-century quest also held an anti-Bultmannian position with regard to the necessity of discovering the historical Jesus. Joachim Jeremias, the scholar who has been perhaps most successful in continuing the attempt to discover the historical Jesus, set forth a position on the significance of the historical Jesus for faith that stood in striking contrast to that of Bultmann. Crucial for understanding Jeremias's theological position is his small book, *The Problem of the Historical Jesus.* In a section entitled "The Necessity of Historical Study," he made two points about the significance of the historical Jesus for faith. First, the gospels testify that the or-

---

[63]Rudolf Bultmann, *Theology of the New Testament,* 2 vols., trans. Kendrick Grobel (New York: Charles Scribner's Sons, 1951-1955) 1:3.

[64]See Fritz Buri, *How Can We Still Speak Responsibly of God?* trans. Charley D. Hardwick (Philadelphia: Fortress Press, 1968 [1967]); *Theology of Existence,* trans. Harold H. Oliver and Gerhard Onder (Greenwood SC: Attic Press, 1965 [1954]); *Christian Faith in our Time,* trans. Edward Allen Kent (New York: Macmillan, 1966 [1952]). Buri, in a play on Bultmann's term demythologizing, used the term dekerygmatizing *(Entkerygmatisierung).*

[65]Schubert Ogden, *Christ Without Myth: A Study Based on the Theology of Rudolf Bultmann* (New York: Harper and Brothers, 1961); see also "Debate on Demythologizing," *Journal of Bible and Religion* 27 (January 1959): 17-27; and Ogden's introduction in *Existence and Faith: Shorter Writings of Rudolf Bultmann,* trans. Schubert Ogden (Cleveland: World 1960).

[66]Karl Jaspers and Rudolf Bultmann, *Myth and Christianity,* trans. N. Gutermann (New York: Noonday Press, 1958 [1953, 1954]).

igin of Christianity centers around a historical figure, Jesus of Nazareth. Second, the kerygma of the early church also refers to the historical Christ event. For Jeremias,

> study of the historical Jesus and his message is no peripheral task of New Testament scholarship, a study of one particular historical problem among many others. It is *the* central task of New Testament scholarship.[67]

That last sentence is almost certainly an allusion to Bultmann's opening sentence in his *Theology of the New Testament* that the message of Jesus is a presupposition, but not a part of, the theology of the New Testament. The first volume of Jeremias's *New Testament Theology*[68] was subtitled *The Proclamation of Jesus,* and its subject matter (the message of the historical Jesus) was a further testimony to the difference between his approach and that of Bultmann.

T. W. Manson never articulated his understanding of the significance of the historical Jesus for faith as carefully as Jeremias. He was however, clearly oriented in a direction similar to that of Jeremias, and his dissatisfaction with Bultmann's theological perspective is evident throughout his writings. Manson never wrote a theology of the New Testament. He did indicate that the historical Jesus and his teachings are the foundation of New Testament theology.[69] Presumably, if he had written such a theology, it would have been organized, like that of Jeremias, around the historical Jesus.

If two extreme positions can be identified in a theological discussion, then someone usually proposes a mediating stance. Although not on the absolute extreme end of the spectrum, Bultmann certainly advocated a position much different from that of Jeremias and Manson with respect to the significance of the historical Jesus for faith. The most significant mediating stance was inaugurated among some of Bultmann's students. Like Strauss, Bultmann, Jeremias, Manson, and others, the theological position of Bultmann's students with respect to the significance of the historical Jesus had its counterpart in their position on the possibility of arriving at knowledge of the historical Jesus. This movement, discussed earlier with respect to the latter point, is now designated as the new quest for the historical Jesus.

Ernst Käsemann, generally considered to have inaugurated the new quest, argued that the early church had an interest in the historical Jesus. He reasoned from this observation that it is appropriate for contemporary persons of faith to recognize the necessity for a closer connection be-

---

[67]Joachim Jeremias, *The Problem of the Historical Jesus,* trans. Norman Perrin (Philadelphia: Fortress Press, 1964 [1960]) 20-21.

[68]Jeremias, who died in 1981, never produced the second volume of his theology.

[69]Manson, *The Teaching of Jesus,* 3.

tween the kerygmatic Christ and the historical Jesus, lest a position be adopted in which there is no continuity between the two.[70] Bultmann had, of course, severed the two. This threatened, according to the new questers, to turn Christianity into a mythological religion and Christ into an idea.

Much of what the new questers said along these lines was also stated by Jeremias. Although he was an ally of the new quest, Jeremias was not a quester, if that term is used to refer to a movement stemming from Käsemann's famous address. Jeremias was more conservative than the new questers in his findings about the historical Jesus, and he was not concerned with an existential interpretation of the New Testament, as the new questers were.

An important book in the new quest was the critical analysis of the movement by James M. Robinson, *A New Quest of the Historical Jesus*. The new quest was now possible, according to Robinson, because it sought after Jesus' selfhood and his understanding of existence.[71] One of the main goals of the new quest, then, was to locate parallels between the kerygma and the historical Jesus; or, as it is often stated, to find implicit in Jesus what was explicit in the kerygma.[72]

Another development, different from but not unrelated to the new quest, was the new hermeneutic movement, primarily associated with Ernst Fuchs and Gerhard Ebeling.[73] Fuchs and Ebeling are to be set off from the new quest because they, more than their colleagues, attached their inquiry to a specific theological stance. Continuing the attempt to locate the continuity between the kerygma and the historical Jesus, this movement introduced the notion of a word event. Ebeling used *Wortgeschehen* (literally "word event") and Fuchs used *Sprachereignis* (literally

---

[70]See Ernst Käsemann, "Blind Alleys in the 'Jesus of History' Controversy," in *New Testament Questions of Today*, trans. W. J. Montague (London: SCM Press, 1969 [1965]) 23-65.

[71]James M. Robinson, *A New Quest for the Historical Jesus*, Studies in Biblical Theology 25 (Naperville IL: Alec R. Allenson, 1959) 66-72; see also *A New Quest of the Historical Jesus and Other Essays* (Philadelphia: Fortress Press, 1983).

[72]See James M. Robinson, "The Recent Debate on the New Quest," *Journal of Bible and Religion* 30 (1960): 198-208.

[73]Gerhard Ebeling, *The Nature of Faith*, trans. Ronald G. Smith (Philadelphia: Muhlenberg Press, 1961 [1959]); *Word and Faith*, trans. James W. Leitch (Philadelphia: Fortress Press, 1963 [1960]); *Theology and Proclamation*, trans. John Riches (London: Collins, 1966 [1962]); and *Introduction to a Theological Theory of Language*, trans. R. W. Wilson (Philadelphia: Fortress Press, 1973 [1971]). Ernst Fuchs, *Studies of the Historical Jesus*, trans. Andrew Scobie (London: SCM Press, 1964 [1960]). See also John B. Cobb and James M. Robinson, eds, *The New Hermeneutic* (New York: Harper and Row, 1964); and Paul J. Achtemeier, *Introduction to the New Hermeneutic* (Philadelphia: Westminster Press, 1969).

"language occurrence") as the key. The continuity was that in the kerygma and in Jesus faith was manifested as word event. This continuity was taken one step further with the affirmation that for the believer, who responded to the kerygma, faith became a word event that echoed the faith of Jesus. The importance of language for the new hermeneutic should be stressed. Robinson called it essentially a "movement of language," whose purpose was

> to indicate the positive and indispensable role of language in understanding. Rather than the language being a secondary, distorting objectification of meaning that must be removed to hear the meaning behind the language, the language of the text is regared positively as an interpretative proclamation of the meaning and hence as our indispensable access to it.[74]

Against this background I now turn to Perrin's intellectual pilgrimage with respect to the significance of the historical Jesus for faith. The fundamental issue he dealt with explicitly throughout his work was that of proper method in exegesis of the New Testament. With respect to method, he was a self-conscious exegete, always aware of the method he utilized and its theoretical justification. He was not always as explicit about the motivation for his work. Perhaps that was because he was a biblical scholar rather than a systematic theologian. His explicit statements about his motivation, however, provide a clue to the structure of his work as that progressed throughout his career. The question of the relationship between faith and history is a question that helps to interpret his scholarly pilgrimage. This issue, as it surfaced in his work, might be expressed in terms of a quest for a foundation for faith. In using faith and history as the paradigm with which to interpret his work, it is helpful to view that issue in terms of a continuum.

There are two extreme positions one can take with respect to faith and history. The historicism of much of the nineteenth-century quest for the historical Jesus was predicated on a position represented today by fundamentalist theology. On the other extreme, is the view that history is of no importance for faith. The positions of Buri, Ogden, and Jaspers are examples of this view.

Perrin's scholarly pilgrimage was motivated by a quest for a basis for faith; his pilgrimage can be broadly subsumed under a continuum on which he moved to positions where history was less and less important for faith. In other words he moved from the "right" toward the "left" side of the continuum—yet he never reached the continuum's extreme left. At the end of his career he was beginning to develop a synthesis that would have incorporated the various positions he had held. Furthermore, there was a reciprocal causative relationship between the exegetical methods employed by Perrin and the conclusions he reached by using those meth-

---

[74]Robinson, "Hermeneutic Since Barth," in *New Hermeneutic*, 4, 6-7.

ods. These conclusions had clear implications for his quest for a foundation for faith.

In his early work Perrin provided only a brief sketch of his position concerning the significance of the historical Jesus. In his first published article[75] he responded favorably to the direction that three of Bultmann's students (Käsemann, Günther Bornkamm, and Fuchs), the new questers, were taking the discussion.

> They are, of all scholars, the most inclined to see the influence of the faith and practice of the early church upon the Gospel narratives as we have them. But they are none the less now finding it possible to establish theologically significant things about the historical Jesus. . . . They are *the* kerygmatic theologians; but they are none the less finding that there is an essential relationship between the historical Jesus and the kerygma.[76]

Again, with respect to the significance of the historical Jesus for faith, Perrin appreciated the new quest's modification of Bultmann's position toward a closer connection between faith and history. He followed with a suggestion about the appropriate agenda for future research. It is "imperative," he wrote "that theologicans should direct their attention to the historical Jesus as a legitimate object of Christian faith and a first concern of Christian theology."[77] This statement echoed Jeremias's judgment that the study of the historical Jesus and his message was "*the* central task of New Testament scholarship."[78] Although brief, Perrin's first article, and especially this sentence, is most important because it reflects his view on this crucial issue at the beginning of his scholarly pilgrimage. He was clearly beginning his career from a conservative (though hardly fundamentalist) position that emphasized the importance of the historical Jesus for faith. This initial position is best viewed as a result of the influence on his thinking of the work of his two early teachers, Manson and Jeremias.

If one believes that a knowledge of the historical Jesus is a basis for faith, then it becomes necessary to obtain such knowledge. It is not at all surprising, then, to find Perrin soon engaged in a determined effort to "rediscover" a significant aspect of the historical Jesus—namely, his teaching. In this effort, which culminated in *Rediscovering*, he made use of the one method, form criticism, that was available to him and that could serve his theologically motivated historical concern. In his form-critical

---

[75]Perrin, "Kerygmatic," written with William R. Farmer. A second article, "The Challenge of New Testament Theology Today," *Criterion* 4 (Spring 1965): 25-34, treated briefly the same issue of the significance of the historical Jesus. By the time "Challenge" was written, however, Perrin had moved to a position more reflective of his later work in *Redicovering*.

[76]Perrin, "Kerygmatic," 96.

[77]Ibid., 97.

[78]Jeremias, *Problem of the Historical Jesus*, 21.

study, he sharpened the criteria for determining authentic saying of Jesus and utilized these criteria to do just that. His form-critical treatment of the synoptic gospels provided him with some knowledge of the historical Jesus. Yet this study also demonstrated to him that the early church absolutely and completely identified the risen Lord of her experience with the earthly, historical Jesus. As a result of this identification, it was very difficult for him to arrive at a knowledge of the historical Jesus.

While a conservative view about the historical basis of faith may have initially motivated Perrin to do form criticism, his form-critical findings could not sustain a conservative position. Such findings forced him into a new position reflected in the rather explicit statement that the "main source [for faith] will always be the proclamation of the Church, a proclamation arising out of a Christian experience of the risen Lord."[79] Although the "main source" for faith was the kerygma, Perrin went on to reflect more specifically on how knowledge of the historical Jesus related to faith. The most extended discussion of this question in all his work is found in the last chapter of *Rediscovering*, where he proposed that one think about three different kinds of knowledge.

Historical knowledge was what could be determined about what actually happened. Historical knowledge could, theoretically, be obtained about any figure or event from the past. This type of factual knowledge often changed as new discoveries were made and better research methods were developed. Any historical knowledge that became significant for the present was what Perrin called historic knowledge. Historic knowledge was possible when some point of contact, such as an understanding of existence, was made between the past figure or event and the present person. An artist challenged by the symbols of primitive art was given as an example of how past historical knowledge became historic knowledge. Finally, faith-knowledge referred to knowledge of some figure or event that became meaningful at the level of religious belief. This knowledge, however, did not have to be historical knowledge. It could be historical knowledge, but it could also be myth or legend. Faith-knowledge introduced that which is beyond history—God and God's activity. For the Christian, faith-knowledge was knowledge of Jesus that was related to the confession of him as Christ and Lord.[80]

In his discussion of the faith-knowledge of Jesus, Perrin introduced what he called the faith-image of Jesus. The content of the faith-image came from traits of the historical Jesus and the historic Jesus. This faith-image was distinguished from the historical Jesus although knowledge of the historical Jesus could be a part of it. It was distinguished because the origin of and basis of the faith-image was really proclamation and not research. "What gives this faith-image validity" he wrote,

---

[79]Perrin, *Rediscovering*, 244.

[80]Ibid., 234ff.

is the fact that it grows out of religious experience and is capable of mediating religious experience; that it develops in the context of the complex mixture of needs, etc., which originally created and continues to create, an openness towards the kerygma; and that it can continue to meet those needs.[81]

What, specifically, was the relationship of historical knowledge to faith-knowledge? Perrin contended that historical knowledge could be significant for faith "in that it can contribute to the formation of the faith-image." Faith, he added, "is necessarily faith *in* something" and "in so far as the 'something' is 'Jesus,' historical knowledge can help to provide the content, without thereby becoming the main source of that content." For Perrin the "main source" for faith would "always be the proclamation of the Church, a proclamation arising out of a Christian experience of the risen Lord." Perrin was prepared to admit fully "the highly individualistic character of a believer's faith-image" while recognizing that interpreters must "face the question of which, if any, are to be called 'Christian.' " He reserved "the right to appeal to our limited, but real, historical knowledge of Jesus," for, he argued, "the true kerygmatic Christ, the justifiable faith-image, is that consistent with the historical Jesus."[82] Following Kähler's much earlier distinction between the historical and the historic Jesus, Perrin, in his delineation of three kinds of knowledge, further refined Kähler's terminology. Like Kähler, he affirmed that it was the kerygmatic Christ and not the historical Jesus that was the basis of faith. At this point Perrin was also in conscious agreement with Bultmann who, in essential agreement with Kähler, had affirmed that the object of faith was the Proclaimed (Kähler's historic Christ) rather than the Proclaimer (Kähler's historical Jesus). Although the object of faith was the Proclaimed, the kerygmatic Christ, Bultmann asserted that the saving event presupposed the "thatness" of Jesus.[83]

Perrin used Bultmann's position, with which he identified, to assess various other attempts to discuss the significance of the historical Jesus. He gave representative examples of positions to the right, left, and center of that of Bultmann. From the right came the claim that the historical nature of the Judeo-Christian faith and the incarnation meant that more emphasis should be put on the historical Jesus than Bultmann did. Jeremias was Perrin's example of a scholar taking this approach. To use Perrin's terminology, Jeremias argued that historical knowledge was directly related to faith-knowledge. From the left came Ogden and Jaspers (Perrin

---

[81]Ibid., 243, 244.

[82]Ibid., 244.

[83]Ibid, 220-21. See also Van A. Harvey's discussion of "Faith and Fact in the Theology of Rudolf Bultmann" in *The Historian and the Believer* (New York: Macmillan, 1966) 139-46.

did not discuss Buri). Both thinkers were similar in affirming that Bultmann was inconsistent when he declared that what was important for faith was the kerygmatic Christ and then maintained a necesssary link with the historical "thatness" of Jesus. Ogden and Jaspers completely severed historical knowledge from faith-knowledge, according to Perrin.[84]

From the center, the new quest of the historical Jesus emphasized the significance of the parallels between the historical Jesus and the church's kerygma. Perrin's criticism of the new quest was that it abandoned the distinction between faith-knowledge and historic by viewing faith-knowledge as historic knowledge. The new quest moved the discussion to the right, in the direction of Jeremias, a direction Perrin disapproved.[85] It is interesting to compare his assessment of the new quest in his first published article with his assessment in *Rediscovering*. In "Kerygmatic" he viewed the new quest from a conservative perspective similar to that of Jeremias, applauding the direction in which the new questers took the discussion. By the time he wrote *Rediscovering* Perrin had moved to a position more compatible with that of Bultmann. From this perspective he criticized the new quest, which he saw as moving away from Bultmann's perspective.

Perrin's early views about the primary concern of Christian theology had become a mandate to "rediscover" the historical Jesus. That task proved very difficult, given the nature of the sources, and led him to reflect explicitly on the significance of the historical Jesus for faith and to reformulate his understanding of such significance. In light of that reformulation he wrote, probably alluding to statements in his first published article, that

> We are not going back to the concept of the historical Jesus as the central concern of Christian faith, nor can we rest content with a faith concerned only with the "kerygmatic Christ," because neither alternative would do justice to the early identification of earthly Jesus and risen Lord. Exactly how we shall ultimately be able to define the true "object" of Christian faith it is too soon to say; but we shall have to do justice to the new understanding of the nature of the synoptic tradition in our discussion, that much is clear. Further, as our historical knowledge of Jesus accumulates, it will inevitably be used in various ways to give content to, to correct, or to interpret our knowledge and understanding of the Lord we experience and proclaim.[86]

This pregnant statement summarized the basic position of Perrin on this issue in his form-critical phase. His theology gave rise to the use of a method which in turn prompted him to reformulate his theology. His

---

[84]Perrin, *Rediscovering*, 223-25; 239.

[85]Ibid., 229-34; 242-43.

[86]Perrin, "Wredestrasse," 300.

continuing investigation of the sources and his new theological under-standing of the significance of the historical Jesus eventually led to what can be termed a new phase in his pilgrimage. Before turning to that new phase, some comments are in order about the ambiguity in his formula-tion in *Rediscovering* as well as a basic weakness of his position.

Although he discussed in detail the significance of the historical Jesus for faith, Perrin's position is somewhat ambiguous. He carefully distin-guished between historical knowledge, historic knowledge, and faith-knowledge. Faith-knowledge, he said, did not have to be historical knowledge.[87] Historical knowledge "can"—but not necessarily does—contribute to the formation of the faith-image that constitutes faith-knowledge. Yet, he stated that the justifiable faith-image was consistent with the historical Jesus.[88] It was at this point that the ambiguity arose. Was Perrin saying that the historical Jesus, is to some degree, the basis of faith or not? It seems that he attempted to answer both in the affirmative and in the negative.[89] That criticism has also been made about the posi-tion of Perrin's mentor, Bultmann. Ogden and Jaspers suggested that Bultmann was inconsistent when he stressed that the kerygmatic Christ was the basis for faith and then maintained the importance of the "that-ness" of Jesus.

Although Perrin's view can be seen as ambiguous, there is another way to understand his formulation. His "position" in *Rediscovering* indicates of the direction in which he was moving relative to the significance of the historical Jesus. His insistence that the faith-image be consistent with the historical Jesus and his concern for arriving at authentic words of Jesus were a reflection of the influence of the conservative position he had ad-vocated in his first published article. His insistence that faith-knowledge was to be distinguished from historical knowledge and that historical knowledge did not necessarily contribute to the faith-image reflected the direction in which he was moving.

Perrin's struggle with the historical Jesus was related to the broader question of the nature and meaning of history. The nineteenth-century quest for the historical Jesus put the emphasis on the facts or events of history. Many theorists today are agreed that history involves to some degree both events and the interpretation of those events.[90] Paul Tillich, for example, argued that history is always a union of objective and sub-jective elements.

---

[87]*Rediscovering*, 235-36.

[88]Ibid., 244.

[89]Erich Grässer, "Norman Perrin's Contribution to the Question of the His-torical Jesus," *Journal of Religion* 64 (October 1984): 498, makes a similar point when he states that Perrin's formulation displays "a certain lack of precision."

[90]See the comment of C. R. North, "History," in *The Interpreter's Dictionary of the Bible*, 5 vols. (Nashville: Abingdon Press, 1962, 1976) 2:607.

All history-writing is dependent both on actual occurrences and on their reception by a concrete historical consciousness. There is no history without factual occurrences, and there is no history without the reception and interpretation of factual occurrences by historical consciousness.[91]

The approach to history reflected in Tillich's statement is the kind of perspective that informed Perrin's formulations about the historical Jesus. Perrin's point that the early church absolutely and completely identified the historical Jesus with the risen Lord was another way of affirming that history is a union of objective and subjective elements. Likewise, his concern to make the kerygmatic Christ the object of faith and yet maintain some link with the historical Jesus was an attempt to keep the objective and subjective elements in balance. This balance, of course, can also be seen as ambiguous—or perhaps more accurately, as reflecting a movement along the continuum.

Along with the ambiguity in Perrin's formulation, there was a basic weakness in its implementation. His position was that historical knowledge of Jesus could be used "to give content to, to correct, or to interpret our knowledge and understanding of the Lord we experience and proclaim."[92] In *Rediscovering* he did basically two things: (1) he utilized form criticism to obtain knowledge of the historical Jesus: and (2) he formulated a position concerning the significance of the historical Jesus for faith. If, as he said, the historical knowledge could contribute in some way to the faith-image, then he should have shown specifically how. He identified a number of emphases in Jesus' Kingdom teaching and the parables. However, he never showed what or how these findings contributed of the faith-image. He simply stated that they did contribute.

This criticism of Perrin is not a criticism directed at his position in principle, but rather one directed at the practice of his program. It is still an important criticism. Unless he were to show how historical knowledge contributed to the faith-image, one could argue that while it is theoretically valid, it is unworkable in practice. For example, how much new historical information is required to make necessary a substantial change in the faith-image? Also, when a faith-image changes, does this change make previous faith-images invalid retroactively? If so, then is not this approach the same as making the historical Jesus the object of faith as Perrin did earlier in his life? These kinds of questions raise issues he did not treat because he neglected to show how his program might work in practice.

One obvious way Perrin could have mitigated this weakness would have been to appropriate something like Bultmann's existentialist inter-

---

[91]Paul Tillich, *Systematic Theology*, 3 vols. (Chicago: University of Chicago Press, 1951-1963) 3:301-302.

[92]Perrin, "*Wredestrasse*," 300.

pretation of the New Testament. Bultmann suggested that there were two kinds of existence: human being outside faith and human being in faith. These corresponded to Heidegger's categories of inauthentic and authentic existence. Existentialist categories were Bultmann's way of bridging the gap between the mythological notions of the New Testament and modernity. Although he was certainly cognizant of Bultmann's approach, Perrin never chose to make these existentialist categories an integral part of his program.

A few comments are in order about the validity of Perrin's movement up to this point in his pilgrimage. His position concerning the significance of the historical Jesus for faith is ambiguous. Yet the direction in which he was moving with respect to the significance of the historical Jesus for faith was appropriate, given the results of his form-critical investigation of the gospels. That Perrin's movement up to this point was appropriate did not mean he could rest here. The ambiguity inherent in his formulation concerning the significance of the historical Jesus for faith meant that he had to continue moving toward a more satisfactory solution with respect to the issue. A movement back to his earlier, more conservative position, where the historical Jesus was an object of faith, was unacceptable for the same reasons charged against the nineteenth-century quest for the historical Jesus—that it was both historically impossible because of the nature of the sources and theologically illegitimate because of the nature of faith and the early church's understanding of history. Because these criticisms were pertinent to his earlier, more conservative position, and to a lesser degree to his position in *Rediscovering*, Perrin had to continue moving to the left side of the continuum. Indeed, he did continue to move in this direction. Whether the future formulations were more acceptable than these earlier formulations is a question to be addressed.

Since form-critical study of the synoptic gospels did not yield a historical Jesus that could serve as the basis for faith, Perrin reformulated his thinking in *Rediscovering* concerning Jesus' significance. The form-critical study had suggested that that kerygma of the early church was of crucial importance, and he took full account of this fact in his theologizing in *Rediscovering*. The view that the historical Jesus could contribute to one's faith-image but was no longer the central concern of faith led him to an acceptance of redaction criticism. This method had been known by Perrin since the 1950s and served his theological interest because of its ability to obtain knowledge about the kerygma of the early church, and in particular the kerygma or theology of the evangelists. Since the kerygma now played a crucial role in his theology, he became an enthusiastic advocate of redaction criticism and an able practitioner of the method.

Two years after his detailed discussion of the significance of the historical Jesus in *Rediscovering*, Perrin returned in *Redaction Criticism* with some brief but important comments on the question. In *Redaction Criticism* he discussed the issue in light of the findings of this method. The critical question was "whether the view of the historical Jesus as the locus of revelation and the central concern of Christian faith is in fact justifiable."[93] In *Rediscovering*, he had to address this question because it was becoming increasingly clear that much of what was in the gospels was to be attributed to the period of oral tradition after the Jesus event. The basic question had not changed. The success of the redaction-critical approach made the question all the more acute. Redaction criticism, Perrin wrote,

> makes clear the fact that the voice of the Jesus of the Gospels is the voice of living Christian experience, and that the evangelists and the tradition they represent are indifferent as to whether this experience is ultimately related to anything said or done in Galilee or Judea before the crucifixion. In light of this fact it seems very hard indeed to justify a Life of Jesus theology. If the Jesus of the Gospel of Mark is the Jesus of Mark's own Christian experience and that of the church before him, then the claim that the "historical" Jesus is the center and source of Christian faith would seem to have no necessary basis in the New Testament. It has always been clear that neither Paul, John, nor the Catholic epistles have the kind of attitude toward the earthly Jesus that would justify a central place for the historical Jesus in Christian theology. It is no accident that the rise of a Life of Jesus theology was closely connected with an acceptance of the Marcan hypothesis. In destroying the Marcan hypothesis redaction criticism would seem to have cut the ground from under the feet of that theology.[94]

By "Marcan hypothesis" Perrin meant the notion that Mark was a reliable historical source for knowledge of the historical Jesus. In a more positive vein he argued that redaction criticism helped to indicate the nature of a "gospel." In doing this it had a positive impact for faith in two ways. First, redaction criticism showed that the "locus of revelation was not the ministry of the historical Jesus but the reality of Christian experience." Second, there was a "real continuity" between the present experience and the past historical Jesus.[95] This latter point was an echo of his position in *Rediscovering*. While he had not previously said so explicitly that the locus of revelation was in Christian experience, this too was consistent with his discussion of the faith-image in *Rediscovering*.[96]

Again, in what was essentially a restatement of his discussion in *Rediscovering* Perrin set forth three different kinds of knowledge. In *Rediscovering* he had called them historical, historic, and faith knowledge. In *Introducton* he called them history as the historical, the historic, and the historicity of human existence in the world. From the perspective of the three kinds of knowledge or history, he developed his understanding of

---

[93]Perrin, *Redaction Criticism*, 72.

[94]Ibid., 74.

[95]Ibid., 75, 79.

[96]See Perrin, *Rediscovering*, 244.

the relationship between myth and history in the New Testament. That myths distorted the historical in the New Testament was clear. When the distortion had to do with historical details that were simply the expressions of the myth, it did not affect the functioning adequacy of the myth as myth. But in some New Testament myths it was claimed that the myth's central figure "exemplified the reality that the myth claims to mediate." If research should show that this central figure did not exemplify this reality, then it would be difficult to accept the myth. This was the element of correlation. For example, the details of the passion story could be proven false by research and the myth would still function. But, Perrin asked, "What if it could be shown that Jesus was carried to the cross railing against God and fate.?" In that case, he responded, the myth "would surely become difficult to accept," since "the claim that Jesus exemplified the myth in his own life, which brings an aspect of the myth into the realm of history as the historical, would in fact be false.[97]

Perrin then pointed out that the myths were used to interpret the history. For example, "The birth of Jesus did change forever the possibilities for a man living in the world; his ascension is a way of saying that there is now a futurity for human existence in the world that there was not before." The ground was now prepared for him to suggest that history itself functioned as myth in the New Testament. "If the myth interprets history" he wrote," we can now claim that the history narrated in the New Testament is history as the historic." For Perrin, then, "history as the historic necessarily involves history as the historical and the historical as interpreted by myth. To speak of history as the historic is to speak of the narration of events that brings out the significance of those events for future generations."[98]

Perrin's position with respect to the significance of the historical Jesus can be set in perspective by noting that he treated the Jesus material in a final chapter of his *Introduction*, "The Presupposition of the New Testament: Jesus." He consciously treated Jesus last. As he explained at the beginning of his textbook,

> It is normal to begin a survey of the New Testament with Jesus—that is, with the historical Jesus—and then go on to examine developments in the later church, understanding those developments as moving forward from the mission and message of the historical Jesus. This was the present writer's own understanding until he was confronted by the work of the German New Testament scholar Rudolf Bultmann. Bultmann begins his *Theology of The New Testament* with the sentence, "The message of Jesus is a presupposition for the theology itself. . . . " Over the years I have wrestled with this problem and am finally convinced that Bultmann is right.

---

[97]Perrin, *Introduction*, 30.

[98]Ibid., 32, 33.

> Hence, in this book the chapter on Jesus is the last chapter and not the first, and the title of that chapter is a deliberate allusion to Bultmann's phase.[99]

It seems that Perrin at this point misinterpreted Bultmann, who, in his *Theology of The New Testament*, began with a chapter on the message of the historical Jesus.[100] What Perrin was doing, in effect, was taking Bultmann's position to its logical conclusion. This was another instance of his extremist approach to New Testament issues, which in this case was moving him toward an ahistorical view of the basis of faith.

Perrin's discussion of the three different kinds of history was another way of affirming that the locus of revelation was Christian experience while still maintaining that there was some continuity between this present experience and the past history of Jesus. Treating the historical Jesus at the end, rather than the beginning, of *Introduction* reflected this same understanding—that what was crucial was the response of early Christianity to the Easter Christ rather than the event of the historical Jesus.

In a most revealing section of *Redaction Criticism*, Perrin provided insight into the motivation for his redaction-critical work. "The real cutting edge of the impact of redaction criticism," he wrote,

> is the fact that it raises very serious questions indeed about that which normally motivates Life of Jesus research: Life of Jesus theology. It raises above all the question as to whether the view of the historical Jesus as the locus of revelation and the central concern of Christian faith is in fact justifiable.[101]

Perrin had now made a definite progression from his understanding of the significance of the historical Jesus at the beginning of his career. Presumably, if he had written a textbook introduction to the New Testament at that point, he would have begun, like Jeremias, with the historical Jesus, whom he then considered "all-important" to faith. This consideration carried over into the next stage of his work and was the motivation for his form-critical analysis of the synoptic gospels. The purpose of his work in *Rediscovering* was to come as close as possible to "hard" knowledge of the historical Jesus. Although he was attempting to get back to knowledge of Jesus because it was important for faith, his earlier conservatism was tempered in *Rediscovering*. Here he was moving very close to Bultmann's position when he argued that the main source for faith is the kerygma.

---

[99]Ibid., 5

[100]Under the chapter title, "The Message of Jesus," Bultmann discussed the eschatological message, Jesus' interpretation of the demand of God, Jesus' idea of God, and the question of the messianic consciousness of Jesus; see *Theology of the New Testament*, 1:3-32.

[101]Perrin, *Redaction Criticism*, 72.

Perrin maintained connection with his early work by suggesting that historical knowledge of Jesus could contribute to faith by contributing to the formation of the "faith-image." While this was a definite shift in emphasis from the early period, his views as expressed in articles from his redaction-critical work confirmed this shift and stated explicitly that the "locus of revelation is not in the ministry of the historical Jesus but the reality of Christian experience." This affirmation was consistent with placing the discussion of the historical Jesus at the end of *Introduction* rather than at the beginning. Continuity between *Rediscovering* and this most recent redaction-critical position was also demonstrated by his affirmation that there was a "real continuity" between the present experience and the past historical Jesus.[102]

---

[102]Ibid., 75, 79.

THE AMERICAN
REFORMULATION:
LITERARY CRITICISM

• From New Criticism to Hermeneutical Process. •

One of the most recent approaches to the study of the gospels has been literary criticism—the application to the gospels of critical princples drawn from modern, general literary criticism. A distinction is made between this newer form of literary criticism of the gospels and the study of sources of the gospels which, among historical critics of the Bible, has also been termed literary criticism. Robert W. Funk called the newer form of criticism "literary literary criticism" to distinguish it from the older literary criticism,[1] which more precisely is and, for sake of clarity, should be called "source criticism.[2]

Several factors contributed to the rise of literary criticism among biblical scholars. One was the natural movement, or what Dan O. Via, Jr., called the "mutation,"[3] of redaction criticism into literary criticism. Form criticism was concerned with the tradition of Jesus material as that material developed through the oral period between the time of Jesus and the written gospels. Redaction criticism was concerned with the way that tradition was redacted and new material was composed by the evangel-

---

[1]Robert W. Funk, "Literary Critical Study of Biblical Texts," *Semeia* 8 (1970): viii.

[2]For discussions of terminology, see Edgar Krentz, *The Historical-Critical Method*, Guides to Biblical Scholarship, ed. Gene M. Tucker (Philadelphia: Fortress Press, 1975) 49-50; and Norman R. Petersen, *Literary Criticism for New Testament Critics*, Guides to Biblical Scholarship, ed. Dan O. Via, Jr. (Philadelphia: Fortress Press, 1978) 10.

[3]Dan O. Via, Jr., "Review of *Introduction*," *Journal of Religion* 55 (October 1975): 459.

ist. While redaction criticism moved a step closer to a focus on the text as it stands, it failed to appreciate fully the final form of the text because of its concern to separate tradition from redaction and to investigate the *Sitz im Leben* of the evangelist. Literary criticism attempted to do full justice to a text as a text, something redaction criticism only partially achieved.

Norman R. Petersen drew on metaphors used by literary critic Murray Krieger[4] to describe the movement of redaction criticism into literary criticism. "By basing their method on the distinction between redacton and tradition," Petersen noted, "redaction critics are forced to look *through* the text by focusing on the relations between it and its sources." Therefore, redaction critics "cannot look *at* the text in order to see, for example, how the units in their linear sequence are related to one another to form the whole." Rather, critics using this method "remain bound to the genetic sequence of stages in textual formation by construing texts as *windows* opening on the pre-literary history of their parts rather than as *mirrors* on whose surfaces we find self-contained worlds." In a positive vein, Petersen concluded,

> redaction criticism raises the very real problem of having to determine the author's investment in each word, sentence, and unit taken over from his sources. Negatively, however, its methodological and theoretical orientation requires us to focus on something other than the text itself. Redaction criticism's concern for composition and authors thus leads to literary problems that it is not designed to deal with.[5]

A second, and perhaps more important factor contributing to the rise of biblical literary criticism, is the way biblical literary critics were increasingly becoming acquainted with and utilizing interpretative principles drawn from modern, nonbiblical literary criticism. The acquaintance with and use of secular literary criticism by biblical scholars was a part of a broader contemporary trend in biblical studies. Patrick Henry, in a recent book surveying new directions in the field, noted that "the migration of biblical study from theological seminaries to religious studies departments in colleges and universities during the past two decades has been rapid and extensive."[6] I should add that such a migration has also been extremely significant for the development of method in biblical studies. As Karlfried Froehlich has pointed out,

> the critical study of the Bible under the auspices of professional societies, the Council on the Study of Religion, and the university departments of religion has been flourishing, reaching out in more and more directions,

---

[4]Murray Krieger, *A Window to Criticism: Shakespeare's Sonnets and Modern Poetics* (Princeton NJ: Princeton University Press, 1964) 3.

[5]Petersen, *Literary Criticism*, 19.

[6]Patrick Henry, *New Directions in New Testament Study* (Philadelphia: Westminster Press, 1979) 20.

and applying freely the insights of sociology, anthropology, psychology, modern linguistics, and other branches of knowledge with their appropriate methodologies to the biblical texts.[7]

Literary criticism of the Bible, a good example of the recent interdisciplinary trend, usually drew upon, while modifying, an American school of nonbiblical literary criticism known as the New Criticism. A brief account of the theory and techniques of the New Criticism, as well as some reasons for its ascendancy and some criticisms of it, is crucial for understanding the methodological milieu out of which biblical literary criticism arose.

As a movement, the beginning of the New Criticism can be traced to the publication from 1922-1925 in Nashville of a magazine of poetry entitled *The Fugitive.* The persons who contributed poems to the magazine, most of whom were associated in some way with Vanderbilt University, included John Crowe Ransom, Allen Tate, Robert Penn Warren, and Cleanth Brooks, Jr.[8] Following the termination of the magazine, these "Fugitives" went on to publish and teach what eventually came to be referred to as the New Criticism. It has also been labeled, for reasons that will become clear, analytical, formalist, and aesthetic criticism.[9] Many other theorists and writers, especially poets, identified with the New Criticism as it became a major force in the study of literature in America in the 1930s and 1940s. *The Southern Review,* established in 1935 at Louisiana State University with Warren and Brooks as editors, was for several years an important outlet for many of the New Critics.

The eventual development of New Critical principles owed much to I. A. Richards's *Practical Criticism.*[10] Richards's aim was to "provide a new technique for those who wish to discover for themselves what they think and feel about poetry" and "to prepare the way for educational methods more efficient than those we use now in developing discrimination and the power to understand what we hear and read."[11] To demonstrate his method Richards interpreted eleven poems, emphasizing the role of me-

---

[7]Karlfried Froehlich, "Biblical Hermeneutics on the Move," *Word & World* 1 (Spring 1981): 140.

[8]See John M. Bradbury, *The Fugitives: A Critical Account* (Chapel Hill: University of North Carolina Press, 1958) 4; see also C. Hugh Holman, "The Defense of Art: Criticism Since 1930," in *The Development of American Literary Criticism,* ed. Floyd Stovall (Chapel Hill: University of North Carolina Press, 1955) 231ff.

[9]See William Van O'Conner, *An Age of Criticism: 1900-1950* (Chicago: Henry Regnery, 1952) 156; William J. Handy, *Kant and the Southern Critics* (Austin: University of Texas Press, 1963) vii; Bradbury, *Fugitives,* 102-103.

[10]I. A. Richards, *Practical Criticism: A Study of Literary Judgment* (New York: Harcourt, Brace and World, 1929).

[11]Ibid., 3.

ter, diction, metaphor, and other such features in providing the meaning of the poem. Because of Richards's concern for the effect a poem had on a reader, a concern referred to as the "affective fallacy" and scorned by the New Critics, Richards is best viewed as a forerunner of the development of New Critical theory.[12] Richards's significance for the New Criticism was that his critical energy was directed to an analysis of the literary features of the text of the poem itself.

In 1937 Ransom, the major impetus behind *The Fugitive* magazine, published an essay, "Criticism, Inc.," which has been called a "clarion call for the New Criticism."[13] Here Ransom scorned philosophers, English professors, and even authors for not providing true criticism of literature. He appealed for a new approach that would move beyond the accumulation of historical, sociological, and biographical data about literature and to a concern for and interest in the "precious object" of literature itself. The meaning of a poem is not found in its cause, but rather in the poem itself, and criticism should reflect this fact.

One year later, two of the original Fugitives, Brooks and Warren, collaborated to write *Understanding Poetry*, one of the most influential textbooks produced by the New Critics. *Understanding Poetry* taught students to concern themselves primarily with the dynamic properties and internal structure of a poem. The authors strove to ascertain what made a poem aesthetically valuable, regardless of its historical context. *Understanding Poetry*, as did much of Brooks's other theoretical and exegetical work, stressed two things: the centrality of irony, paradox, and other such literary techniques in interpretation; and the necessity to concentrate critical energy on the poem as a self-sufficient, organic whole, not as a combination of elements.[14] Commenting on the significance of *Under-*

---

[12]One of the best discussons of Richards' works is John Crowe Ransom, *The New Criticism* (Norfolk CT: New Directions, 1941) 3ff., esp. 44ff.; See also O'Conner, *Age of Criticism*, 168ff. Richards's "affective fallacy" was discussed, for example, by Ransom in his chapter on Richards (3ff). Ransom later admitted an emotive element into his own critical theory, as was pointed out by Bradbury, *Fugitives*, 144.

[13]John Crowe Ransom, "Criticism, Inc.," included in Ransom, *The World's Body* (New York: Charles Scribner's Sons, 1938); cf. Thomas Daniel Young, "The Evolution of Ransom's Critical Theory: Image and Idea," in Young, ed., *The New Criticism and After* (Charlottesville: University Press of Virginia, 1976) 23.

[14]See Cleanth Brooks and Robert Penn Warren, *Understanding Poetry* (New York: Henry Holt and Co., 1938); cf. Bradbury, *Fugitives*, 233. Several years later Brooks and Warren again collaborated to write *Understanding Fiction* (New York: F. S. Crofts, 1943) in an attempt to apply the New Criticism to fiction. This book, though important and widely used, was never as popular as *Understanding Poetry*. Brooks elaborated upon the New Critical principles used in his earlier works in *The Well Wrought Urn: Studies in the Structure of a Poem* (New York: Regnal and Hickcock, 1974).

standing Poetry for the New Critical movement, John M. Bradbury cited "the consistent focus" of the authors on "the whole poem, seen as a self-sufficient entiry—not as a combination of elements, but as an organic thing in which every element is integral." "For the first time in textbook history," Bradbury observed, "a valid objective method for introducing poetry to the common reader was offered in this book, and its effect on teaching faculties and on subsequent writers of poetry texts was immense."[15]

In 1941 Ransom wrote *The New Criticism*, a book that gave the New Criticism its name and provided the first history of the movement. But in Ransom's more theoretical work, *The World's Body*, he attempted to set forth a coherent system of poetics that did justice to the literary object under study. The central theme of the New Critics, at this time becoming common, was again stressed. "The students of the future," Ransom wrote, "must be permitted to study literature, and not merely about literature."[16]

A good example of the New Criticism at work was *How Does a Poem Mean?*, by John Ciardi and Miller Williams, a widely used textbook in poetry courses. In teaching poetry, the authors of *How Does a Poem Mean?* emphasized a careful reading of the poem rather than on information about the poet's life or on the historical situation out of which the poem came. In their view, when the student has been taught to identify the basic elements of poetry like diction, metaphor, rhythm, and so on, "he will have identified the poem in action. He will not need to fumble at the question *'What* does this poem mean?' He will, rather, have experienced it as a performance. He will have seen *how* it means."[17] In a style typical of New Critics Ciardi and Williams criticized Robert Frost's "Stopping by Woods on a Snowy Evening" to illustrate how a poem means. This 16-line poem elicited seven pages of analysis from the authors. Their close reading was concerned not with the biography of Frost or the historical situation of the text, but rather with the pattern of the poem, the movement of the characters, and the use of foils, symbols, repetition, rhyme, and other aesthetic techniques.[18]

As David Robertson summed up the main tenets of the New Criticism, it is

> principally concerned with the text as it presents itself to the reader. The
> hallmark of this type of criticism is "close reading," the meticulous, de-

---

[15]Bradbury, *Fugitives*, 233.

[16]Ransom, *World's Body*, 455. For a discussion of Ransom as critic, see Bradbury, *Fugitives*. Ransom's poetry is discussed by Bradbury on 15-48.

[17]John Ciardi and Miller Williams, *How Does a Poem Mean?* 2nd ed. (Boston: Houghton Mifflin, 1975 [1959]) xxii.

[18]Ibid., 6-13.

tailed analysis of the verbal texture of the work paying particular attention to patterns of imagery, use of metaphors and the type of interplay between words that generates wit, paradox, and irony. These critics emphasize the way the verbal interrelations within the text work together to produce an organic whole that is more than the addition of the parts.[19]

One way to better understand the New Criticism is to view it in part as a revolt against a more historical approach to literature in vogue in the early part of this century. Much pre-New Criticism criticism was concerned with analyzing the historical, political, and social factors that brought a text into being. These factors were determinative of the way the text was interpreted. Integral to the New Critical discussions of the theory of criticism was a disdain for this "genetic fallacy." In the judgment of Allen Tate, one of the Fugitives,

> the historical approach to criticism, in so far as it has attempted to be a scientific method, has undermined the significance of the material which it proposes to investigate. On principle the sociological and historical scholar must not permit himself to see in the arts meaning that his method does not assume. What the scholars are saying, of course, is that the meaning of a work of literature is identical with their method of studying it—a method that dissolves the literature into its history. Are the scholars studying literature, or are they not? That is the question. If they are not, why then do they continue to pretend that they are?[20]

In their rebellion against historical criticism, the New Critics converged on the "intentional fallacy" of many literary critics. Intentional fallacy refers to the centering of the critical process on the intention of the author. If the text is a self-sufficient, organic whole that can stand alone, then the intention of the original author is of minimal value in determining the meaning of the text.[21]

If the New Critics were unconcerned about the historical factors that gave birth to the text, they were also unconcerned about the effect the text had on its readers. As mentioned earlier, the New Critics criticized the "affective fallacy" of centering the critical process in the psychological reactions or responses the reader or critic made to the text. Emotional effect was not, according to the New Critics, a legitimate subject for criticism because it was too imprecise for careful, objective analysis. At this point

---

[19]Robertson, a professor of English, provided this description of the New Criticism in "Literature, the Bible as," *The Interpreter's Dictionary of the Bible*, 5 vols. (Nashville: Abingdon Press, 1962, 1976) Supp.: 550.

[20]Allen Tate, *Reason in Madness, Critical Essays* (New York: G.P. Putnam's Sons, 1941) 472-75.

[21]For a discussion of the intentional fallacy, see Murray Krieger, *Visions of Extremity in Modern Literatue*, vol. 1 of *The Tragic Vision: The Confrontation of Extremity* (Baltimore: Johns Hopkins University Press, 1973 [1960]) 232.

the New Critics were revolting against what they viewed as an overly impressionistic trend in literary criticism.

This trend was represented by such persons as James Gibbons Huneker (1860-1921), whose writings were characterized by an intuitive, subjective response to art, and by H. L. Mencken (1880-1956), who stressed that art functions to give rise to feelings that then are expressed as art. The New Criticism, then, was basically concerned with the text as an entity in itself, and in particular with the literary elements of the text. It did not ask the question "What did the text mean?" or even "What does the text mean?" Rather, its concern was, as suggested by Ciardi and Williams, "*How* does the text mean?"

Finally, the New Criticism was an approach to art that nullified the old dicotomy of form and content. The New Critics spoke of the "heresy of paraphrase," which separated form and content by attempting to reduce literary work to propositional statements.[22] Because form was viewed as an essential part of the content of a work, a careful analysis of its formal features was necessary for proper understanding. To paraphrase a poem was to destroy it as a poem. William Beardslee has traced the discussion of form and content back to Aristotle.

> Aristotle's *Rhetoric* . . . treats the form as the vehicle for a content which can stand on its own right, apart from the form. Form, from this point of view, becomes simply a means for effectively (persuasively) communicating the content, which in turn is thought of as an idea . . . a second line of tradition, descending from a very much more important work of Aristotle, the *Poetics* . . . regards literary form as an essential part of the function of the work, and not as a separable, instrumental addition to the intellectual content.[23]

The New Criticism, although it has had a great impact on present literary theory, has had its own critics. The basic complaint is that the New Criticism carried internal technical analysis of a text to extreme lengths, thereby ignoring important extraformal factors. The final outcome was to cut the text off from the world, the poet, the reader, and other texts—indeed, from life itself. "When the New Criticism is considered in its historical context, its stress on the autonomy of the text can be seen as a justifiable, and valuable corrective," Lynn Poland has written. "As a complete theory of literature, however, the New Critical program is limited, for the work is, in effect, regarded — as an 'ownerless, unasserted, non-referential, uncredited, and thoroughly insulated something.' " In

---

[22]Bradbury, *Fugitives*, 250.

[23]William A Beardslee, *Literary Criticism of the New Testament*, Guides to Biblical Scholarship, ed. Dan O. Via, Jr. (Philadelphia: Fortress Press, 1970) 3-4. See also J. P. Pritchard, "Aristotle's *Poetics* and Certain American Literary Critics," *Classical Weekly* 27 (January 1934): 81-99.

Poland's terms, "Both the literary text and the reader of the text are de-historicized" by the New Critics, and this imposes sereve limitations on their results.

> By severing literature's ties to its origins in human experience, and by stressing the purely aesthetic being of the emotions and ideas a work includes, the New Criticism cannot explain how literature can give us any knowledge about ourselves and the world. By conceiving the task of criticism to be an understanding of the internal relationships within a text, the New Critics make it difficult to describe how literature does, in fact, extend and transform our perceptions of what it means to be human. The New Criticism, in short, provides us with a poetics, but not a hermeneutics.[24]

The height of the New Critical movement arrived in the 1930s and 1940s when New Criticism became entrenched in literary journals and departments of English. By the mid-1950s new directions in literary criticism were opening up, even among some New Critical advocates. One development was an attempt at a synthesis of the aesthetic emphasis of the New Criticism with the social-historical concerns of an older form of criticism. Perhaps the protype for this development was the textbook, *Theory of Literature*, by René Wellek and Austin Warren.[25] Wellek and Warren treated the text as a thing in itself, but sought to mitigate what was already being viewed as some of the excesses of the New Criticism. They proposed to combine intrinsic criticism (the New Critical emphasis on a close reading of a text) with extrinsic criticism (taking note of the biographical, sociological, psychological, and theological referents in a text). Murray Krieger, who views poems as windows with meaning coming through as well as mirrors with meaning locked in,[26] is a good example of a contemporary literary critic proposing such a synthesis.

---

[24]Lynn Poland, "Literary Criticism of New Testament Narrative: A Literary Critic's Perspective," (unpublished paper, n.d.) 7. Cf. chapter 2, "The Limits of Formalism," in Poland, *Literary Criticism and Biblical Hermeneutics: A Critique of Formalist Approaches*, American Academy of Religion Academy Series 48 (Chico CA: Scholars Press, 1985). Poland's work will be taken up in more detail in the conclusion to the study. See also O'Conner, *Age of Criticism*, 172ff. One of the most developed arguments against the notion that the author's intention does not play a legitimate role in establishing the meaning of a text is in the chapter entitled "In Defense of the Author," in E. D. Hirsch, Jr.'s *Validity in Interpretation* (New Haven CT: Yale University Press, 1967) 1ff. Hirsch argues that the theory of "semantic autonomy" led to "willful arbitrariness and extravagance in academic criticism and has been one very important cause of the prevailing skepticism which calls into doubt the possibility of objectively valid interpretation" (2).

[25]René Wellek and Austin Warren, *Theory of Literature* 3rd. ed. (New York: Harcourt, Brace and World, 1956 [1942]).

[26]Krieger, *Window to Criticism*, 3.

Another development, which Bradbury calls the "newer" New Criticism,[27] turned in the direction of research into myth, ritual, and symbolism and the applicaton of findings from these studies to literary texts. An example of this development is the discussion surrounding the interpretation of symbols. Philip Wheelwright, a philosopher with a keen interest in language, was an ally of the New Criticism in that his concern was to examine the nature and function of symbols as expressive language. Wheelwright defined a symbol as "a relatively stable and repeatable element of perceptual experience, standing for some larger meaning or set of meanings which cannot be given, or not fully given, in perceptual experience itself." Wheelwright stressed the stable and repeatable character of a symbol and said an image "acquires a symbolic nature when, with whatever modifications, it undergoes or is considered capable of undergoing recurrence."[28]

Wheelwright distinguised between two different kinds of symbols. A "steno-symbol" has a one-to-one relationship to that which it represents. One who uses steno-symbols demands that they have a "public exactitude, an uncompromising identity of reference for all who use them correctly." The symbol π is a good example of a steno-symbol. A "tensive symbol" has a set of meanings and no single referent adequately expresses the meaning of the symbol. It "draws life from a multiplicity of associations." There is a "stored up potential of semantic energy and significance which the symbol, when adroitly used, can tap."[29] Wheelwright further defined the two types of symbols in a later book. Tensive symbolism is "expressive" or "depth" language while steno-symbolism is "literal" language. Wheelwright went on to say that "what mainly produces depth-meanings, distinguishing them from steno-meanings, is the greater vivacity of imagination that goes into their making."[30]

Paul Ricoeur, also very interested in semiotics, made a similar distinction, though he used the term "sign" for what Wheelwright called a steno-symbol. A sign is transparent of meaning and is exhausted by its "first or literal intentionality," while a symbol is a sign that points beyond itself to something else.[31] The kind of distinction made by Wheelwright and Ricoeur has been recognized by other literary critics, such as Northrup Frye in *Anatomy of Criticism*,[32] where he made a distinction between

[27]Bradbury, *Fugitives*, 259.

[28]Philip Wheelwright, *Metaphor and Reality* (Bloomington: Indiana University Press, 1962) 2, 32.

[29]Ibid., 94.

[30]Philip Wheelwright, *The Burning Fountain: A Study in the Language of Symbolism*, rev. ed. (Bloomington: Indiana University Press, 1968 [1954]) 3-4, 32.

[31]Paul Ricoeur, *The Symbolism of Evil* (Boston: Beacon Press, 1969) 15.

[32]Northrup Frye, *Anatomy of Criticism: Four Essays* (New York: Atheneum. 1966 [1957]) 73.

a sign that directs the reader's attention outward and a motif that directs the reader's attention inward. Frye referred to both sign and motif as kinds of symbols.

In summary, the New Criticism, in the second quarter of this century, made a substantial alteration in the way a literary text was interpreted by focusing the critic's attention on the text as it stood before the reader. Subsequent modifications of New Critical theory have returned attention to historical referents of the text as well as continued the New Critical emphasis on language with more intensive studies of the nature of symbolic language. It was against the background of the New Criticism and its modifications that a number of contemporary American biblical critics approached the text. Those critics concerned especially with the New Testament included Amos N. Wilder, Robert W. Funk, John D. Crossan, and Dan O. Via, Jr. These critics often attempted literary criticism of the Bible without giving much explicit attention to the theory of the method they used. Attention to some of the theoretical comments they did make is in order.

One of the first major efforts to approach the New Testament from the perspective of the New Criticism was Amos N. Wilder's *Early Christian Rhetoric*, first published in 1964. Wilder, brother of the writer Thornton Wilder, was uniquely prepared to help inaugurate literary criticism of the Bible because he was a poet and literary critic as well as a New Testament scholar. Wilder's debt to the New Critical theory is evident in that he drew heavily on

> literary criticism [where] attention has now for some time been directed to the given work as a self-sufficient aesthetic whole which should be allowed to make its own impact apart from extraneous considerations having to do with the author and his circumstances or intentions or with distinctions between matter and form. The particular "word" of the poem, play, or novel is to be encountered at the level of its own coherent and interrelated pattern of imagery and design. Such a plea for the properly autonomous creation of the artist represents a persuasive protest against that kind of criticism which obscures the unity of the work either by preoccupation with isolated elements or by some didactic concern.[33]

Early Christian Rhetoric was an attempt to bring the New Critical perspective to the New Testament by identifying the major forms and genres of language used by the early church. Chapters were devoted to the dialogue, story, parable, and poem. In concentrating on the literary features of these forms and genres, Wilder's intention was to break down the distinction often made between form and content; he spoke approvingly of the "new appreciation of the inseparable relation of form and content in all texts." "The particular topic," he added, "is not so much what the early

---

[33]Amos N. Wilder, *Early Christian Rhetoric: The Language of the Gospels*, rev. ed. (Cambridge: Harvard University Press, 1971 [1964]) xxv.

Christians said as how they said it. Yet these two matters cannot finally be separated, as every student of literature and art knows."[34] Wilder's basic criticism of the older "Bible as Literature" approach to teaching the Bible in college and university English departments was that it unnaturally separated the Bible into literary/artistic form and religious/theological content.[35] As second major New Critical insight Wilder brought to his study was that attention should be given to the "self-sufficient aesthetic whole," whether it be the whole of a parable or a gospel. He spoke approvingly of redaction criticism, which was moving closer to "a recognition of the total structure of each gospel."[36]

Although *Early Christian Rhetoric* was in many ways a New Critical approach to the New Testament, it was in two important ways a modification of New Critical theory. First, Wilder used the insights of form criticism of the gospels to enable him to understand better the forms and genres of the early church.[37] Second, he appropriated insights from the "new hermeneutic" movement insofar as they help one to "existentially appropriate" the New Testament. These two modifications of the New Critical approach roughly constituted what the New Critics called the intentional and the affective fallacies. The first modification corresponded to a modification of New Criticism made by secular literary critics. The second was a modification that was common among biblical critics who used New Critical principles.

Unlike Wilder, Robert W. Funk did not consciously draw on New Critical principles; but his major work, *Language, Hermeneutic, and Word of God* exhibited a debt to the movement. Funk's concern was to "liberate language" from the past so that the word of God could again enter language and confront man. The first part of Funk's program was certainly a New Critical concern. To bring about the second part of his program, Funk drew heavily on the new hermeneutic and committed what the strict New Critics called affective fallacy. Gerhard Ebeling and Ernst Fuchs were led, Funk observed, "to the conclusion that the word of God is not interpreted—rather it interprets." Funk concluded that "this startling insight" had reversed the "direction of the flow between interpreter and text that has dominated modern biblical criticism from its inception," allowing hermeneutics to become the effort to allow God to address man through the medium of the text."[38] In a more recent book, Funk stated

---

[34]Ibid., xxii, 24.

[35]See Wilder's brief review and critique of the "Bible as Literature" approach in ibid., xii-xxi.

[36]Ibid., xxv.

[37]Ibid., xi.

[38]Robert W. Funk, *Language, Hermeneutic, and Word of God: The Problem of Language in the New Testament and Contemporary Theology* (New York: Harper and Row, 1966) 10-11.

clearly that it is through the form of a text that God addresses human beings. "Subject matter," Funk wrote, "is not something else, to be divorced entirely from words. *What* the parable says cannot be simply divorced from the *way* it says. Form and content are wedded."[39] After his formal analysis of the parable of the leaven (Matthew 13:33), Funk noted, underscoring his concern for the existential confrontation between the text and the interpreter, that "an analysis of this type may turn out to be just one more opinion in the pantheon of opinions, unless or until it throws the interpreter back upon the text and leaves him there in solitude to confront the text without benefit of conceptual comforts."[40]

A major attempt to work out, in light of the New Criticism, a consistent literary approach and to apply that approach to New Testament texts was Dan O. Via's *The Parables*. Via was interested in interpreting the parables and, while he made it clear that his literary approach was especially applicable to the parables because of their aesthetic features, he made no claim that other New Testament texts were as amenable to such analyses.

Via made a distinction between the "through-meaning" and "in-meaning" of language, a distinction similar to the effort to distinguish between different kinds of symbols made by Wheelwright and Ricoeur. Propositional or nonaesthetic language draws primarily on language's through-meaning, while aesthetically developed language, like that of parables, draws primarily on language's in-meaning.[41] An interpretative method appropriate to the kind of language being considered should be used. In the New Critical tradition, Via stressed the unity of form and content and also recognized the autonomy of the aesthetic text.[42] Like most biblical literary critics, he modified the strict New Critical principles. While an aesthetic text has an "in-meaning," Via wrote, "the aesthetically organized form or pattern of connections itself contains implicitly a perspective on life or understanding of existence."

> In a truly aesthetic piece of narrative fiction the centripetal interlocking of the parts will keep the attention focally on the work itself. But the reader will be subsidiarily aware—aware at lower levels of consciousness—of various kinds of pointing outward to the world outside the narrative. . . . The existential understanding is a inherent part of the work. Theological and philosophical views of how and why things happen as they do, if they are fused into the work's internal coherence, are not extra-aesthetic.[43]

---

[39]Robert W. Funk, *Jesus as Precursor*, Society of Biblical Literature *Semeia* Supplement 2, ed. William A. Beardslee (Philadelphia: Fortress Press, 1975) 64.

[40]Ibid., 71.

[41]Dan O. Via, Jr. *The Parables: Their Literary and Existential Dimension* (Philadelphia: Fortress Press, 1967) 73.

[42]Ibid., 75, 77, 78. Via also provided an extended "Critique of the Severely Historical Approach" to interpreting the parables; see 22-24.

[43]Ibid., 82, 87.

In the second half of his book, Via performed his exegesis of a number of Jesus' parables, interpreting each under the three rubrics of historico-literary criticism, literary-existential analysis, and existential-theological interpretation. The first rubric was essentialy a consideration of the historical context of the parable, while the last drew on the new hermeneutic to elucidate the parable's understanding of existence. It was the literary-existential analysis (plot, plot movemet [comic or tragic], dialogue, character activity, and so on) that was the focus of most of Via's attention, the most important step in parable interpretation, and the kind of approach drawn from the New Criticism.

John Dominic Crossan made use of insights and techniques of the New Criticism and urged that literary criticism of the Bible must be given equal room with historical criticism. "Literature reminds history," Crossan wrote in 1976, "that it is language and text that binds the historical student with the historical subject and that it may be terribly naive to ignore that medium in which we all live, move and have our being."[44] In his *In Parables*[45] Crossan had used literary criticism as a way to understand better the teaching of Jesus in its historical expression, a use of literary criticism rather uncommon among biblical critics.

Some comments are now in order concerning the relationship of biblical literary criticism to the historical-critical method, which has dominated most modern study of the Bible. Specifically, is literary criticism as practiced by the biblical literary critics surveyed above another method along the (historical) lines of form and redaction criticism, or is it a method in contradistincton to the historical-critical method?

Of the biblical critics surveyed here, all paid attention—some more than others—to the historical context of the text. Wilder utilized the findings of form critics to identify and discuss the forms of speech and writing of the early church. Via began his exegesis of each parable with historico-literary criticism, which drew essentially on the fruits of historical-critical parable research. Crossan used literary criticism to assist in arriving at the teaching of the historical Jesus. Funk, although less interested in the historical situation, did not completely neglect it. These critics perhaps because of the long historical orientation of biblical studies, did not deny the historical-critical method. However, they all emphasized literary criticism in their work and agreed that interpretation has only just begun when the historical questions have been answered.

While it is clear that these literary critics did not supplant historical criticism, they did move criticism of the Bible away from a historical ori-

---

[44]John Dominic Crossan, *Raid on the Articulate: Comic Eschatology in Jesus and Borges* (New York: Harper and Row, 1976) xiii.

[45]John Dominic Crossan, *In Parables: The Challenge of the Historical Jesus* (New York: Harper and Row, 1973).

entation by introducing an ahistorical (strictly defined) method different from the historically inclined source, form, and redaction-critical methods. Only time will tell whether or not literary criticism (or other ahistorical approaches) will effectively supplant historical-critical approaches in biblical studies. That it is much too early for the verdict to be in can be seen in comments by various critics. Krentz urged that allowance be made for literary criticism (and other methods) as a different, but legitimate, way to read the Bible alongside historical criticism. Petersen attempted to place literary criticism within the context of the historical-critical approach, without watering down the strengths of either. On the other hand, Robertson viewed the increasing use of literary criticism by biblical critics as part of a turning away from history to a concern for language in Western culture.[46] Using "paradigm" as a word to describe "any idea or set of ideas that provides the framework within which a given set of phenomena are understood," Robertson said the paradigm of literary criticism is language and literature as opposed to the paradigm of history that has governed the study of the Bible for more than a hundred years.[47]

Related to the movement, however pronounced, from a historical to a literary paradigm was the shift from a concern for Life of Jesus research to a concern for hermeneutics (the interpretation of written texts). This shift was seen in the evolution of source, form, redaction, and then literary criticism. Both the move to a literary paradigm and the lessening of a concern for Life of Jesus research were also reflected in Perrin's scholarly pilgrimage.

Perrin's struggle to define a proper approach to the New Testament and to assign apropriate terms to the various aspects of the approach was evident in three articles (cited below, in footnotes 48, 49, and 50) published in 1971-1972. In the first article he delineated five aspects of what he called the "hermeneutical task": historical criticism (in the sense of realizing that the documents emerged out of concrete historical situations), literary criticism (the forms and language of the text and the way the forms and language function), the philosophy of language, the insights of the historian of religion, and those of the historian of Christian hermeneu-

---

[46]Krentz, *Historical-Critical Method*, 71; Petersen, *Literary Criticism*, 10-11; Robertson, "Literature, the Bible as," 547.

[47]Robertson, "Literature, the Bible as," 547-48. Other scholars critical of the historical approach have called for a paradigm other than literary criticism. Walter Wink, for example, in *The Bible in Human Transformation: Toward a New Paradigm for Biblical Study* (Philadelphia: Fortress Press, 1973) 1-2, declared that historical criticism of the Bible is "bankrupt" and suggested an approach to the Bible that is based on personal interaction informed by psychotherapeutic principles (19ff.).

tics. Perrin argued that when there was conflict it was historical criticism that exercised normative influence over the others.[48]

In the second article Perrin summarized the various features that should characterize a proper approach to the synoptic gospels and Acts. He termed this general approach "literary criticism"—which, as he used the phase, was synonymous with "method in study and interpretation." The literary critic, he said, must learn from those critics who work on other literature. Literary criticism was now defined as having to do with: textual criticism, source criticism, historical criticism, form criticism, redaction criticism, composition and structure, a concern for protagonists and plot, and themes of the authors. "We are not going to abandon source . . . form and redaction criticism," Perrin wrote. "What I am urging is that we add to these the insights and concerns which stem naturally from the realization that the evangelists are authors."[49]

In the third article Perrin defined the task of interpretation in a slightly different way by setting forth three basic aspects of interpretation: historical criticism, literary criticism, and hermeneutics.[50] "Literary criticism" was not used here as an umbrella term that included all the features of a proper approach (as in the second article). Rather, it was set apart from historical criticism, which was used to refer to the predominant ways the New Testament had been studied in modern research.[51] In addition, hermeneutics was introduced as an important part of the interpretative process.

In these three articles just reviewed, Perrin could use "literary criticism" to mean the form and language of the text[52] or to refer to all methods in study and interpretation.[53] It was the former which Perrin settled on as his work progressed into a stage characterized by a use of literary criticism. He had now moved from an emphasis on redaction criticism to a much more comprehensive understanding of method. The most important development was the introduction of literary criticism into his approach to the New Testament.

---

[48]Norman Perrin, "Towards an Interpretation of the Gospel of Mark," in Hans Dieter Betz, ed., *Christology and a Modern Pilgrimage: A Discussion with Norman Perrin* (Claremont CA: Scholar's Press, 1971) 68-69.

[49]Norman Perrin, "The Evangelist as Author: Reflections on Method in the Study and Interpretation of the Synoptic Gospels and Acts," *Biblical Research* 17 (1972): 10-15.

[50]Norman Perrin, "Historical Criticism, Literary Criticism, and Hermeneutics: The Interpretation of the Parables of Jesus and the Gospel of Mark Today," *Journal of Religion* 52 (October 1972): 362-63.

[51]For example, study of authorship, date, forms, redactions.

[52]As in "Interpretation," 68-69, and "Literary Criticism," 362-63.

[53]As in "Evangelist," 10-15.

Redaction criticism evolved naturally into literary criticism for Perrin because the former took seriously the final form of the text. Via, a practitioner of literary criticism who was happy with the evolution, wrote that Perrin came closer to seeing the gospels as narrative wholes than earlier redaction critics.[54] As Perrin himself recorded this broadening of redaction criticism,

> once it was recognized that the final author was in fact an *author* and not merely a transmitter of tradition, it became natural and inevitable to inquire into his total literary activity as revealing his purpose and theology, not only into his redaction of previously existing tradition. In this connection redaction criticism shades over into general literary criticism, especially in the redaction critical work carried on in America, where the influence of general literary criticism is strong on New Testament scholars.[55]

The broadening of redaction criticism culminated in *Language*, Perrin's last major scholarly work, published in 1976 and dedicated "to Amos Wilder and Paul Ricoeur who taught me to look at the problem of hermeneutics in new ways."[56] The book and the dedication reflected Perrin's openness to an interdisciplinary approach to biblical studies. Wilder was, of course, one of the pioneers in bringing the New Criticism to a study of the New Testament. Ricoeur, who, with Perrin, taught at the University of Chicago, has expertise in several fields, including existentialist and phenomenological philosophy, Freudian psychology, structuralism, and sociology.

Perrin's statements in *Language* on the theory and practice of interpreting the New Testament are important for charting the last stage in his pilgrimage with respect to method. In *Language* he delineated a four-step process which he viewed as applicable to any written text, although in this book his concern was limited to the Kingdom of God and parables in the teaching of Jesus.

The first step in what Perrin called the "hermeneutical process" was textual criticism. Textual criticism is usually understood as referring to the examination of the various manuscripts of a text to determine the most probable reading of the lost autograph. As a historical-critical scholar Perrin had always assumed textual criticism in this sense. In *Language*, however, he expanded the notion of textual criticism to include questions that the form critic asks. For example, in parable research this meant that the critic attempted to determine the authenticity of the sayings attributed to Jesus.[57]

---

[54]Dan. O. Via, "Review of *Introduction*," 459.

[55]Perrin, *Introduction*, 13.

[56]Norman Perrin, *Jesus and the Language of the Kingdom: Symbol and Metaphor in New Testament Interpretation* (Philadelphia: Fortress Press, 1976) v.

[57]Ibid., 2-4.

The second step, closely related to the first, was historical criticism. To Perrin this meant understanding the text as the author intended or as it was understood by those who first read or heard it. He pointed to redaction criticism of the synoptic gospels as the most recent advance in the area of historical criticism.[58] It is not clear why he separated textual criticism and historical criticism in *Language*.[59] In other articles from this phase, he spoke only of historical criticism and placed under this rubric what was called textual criticism in *Language*. In any case, he maintained a respect for the text in its original historical setting, at one point saying failure to do so was committing an "act of rape" on the text.[60] Perrin concluded that he "would never accept a view of hermeneutics which did not see historical criticism as the essential first step in coming to understand any text."[61]

Up to this point, Perrin had merely summarized the historical approach characteristic of his earlier books and articles. What was new in his method was the addition of literary criticism as a crucial step in the hermeneutical process. Literary criticism, according to him, was concerned with "the nature and natural force of both the literary form and language of a text." Taking seriously the literary features of a text meant, for him, paying careful attention to the role of symbol, simile, metaphor, myth, and other such literary features. This kind of literary-critical appreciation for a text could help one gain a better historical understanding of the text. Perrin gave as an example the recognition of the parables of Jesus as parables and not allegories as helping Adolf Jülicher and subsequent scholars to interpret them properly in the life of Jesus.[62] Perrin's concern at this point echoed that of Crossan whose book, *In Parables*, attempted to place the parables in the context of the teaching of Jesus through a literary-critical study of them. Literary criticism for Perrin was not only related to a historical understanding of a text, the first and second steps in the process. It could also contribute to hermeneutics, the fourth and final step in the process.

For this final step in the hermeneutical process, Perrin was indebted to the work of Bultmann. Bultmann believed God encountered humankind in the word. He attempted to remove the obstacle which prevented the hearing of this word. The obstacle to hearing was the New Testament's mythological language. For Bultmann, the notion that death could

---

[58]Ibid., 4-5.

[59]See Perrin, "Eschatology and Hermeneutics: Reflections on Method in the Interpretation of the New Testament," *Journal of Biblical Literature* (March 1974): 4-5; and "Literary Criticism," 362-63.

[60]Perrin, "Literary Criticism," 363.

[61]Perrin, "Eschatology," 5.

[62]Perrin, *Language*, 5, 197-203, 7.

be the atonement for sin and the notion of resurrection were myths that today could not be accepted as true. Humankind could, however, obtain authentic existence in the world when confronted by that of which the New Testament speaks in mythological language. According to Bultmann, the appropriate way to approach the text was with the question of human existence. The gap between the ancient Jewish apocalyptic and the modern interpreter could be bridged because both were concerned with an understanding of life in the world. The reader interacts with the text by questioning it concerning its understanding of human existence. The reader is in turn questioned by the text concerning the possibilities of human existence in the world.

The notion of a dialogue between the text and reader greatly influenced Perrin's formulation. He defined hermeneutics, the final step in his hermeneutical program, as the "dynamic interaction between text and interpreter."[63] Although greatly indebted to his program, Perrin advanced beyond Bultmann's understanding of hermeneutics in one important way—in his attempt to do justice to a text's literary factors and their influence on hermeneutics. "There is a close relationship between literary criticism and hermeneutics," Perrin asserted, "because if a consideration of literary form and type of language is literary criticism, then a consideration of their function, especially of the nature of the response they evoke, is hermeneutics."[64] Bultmann attempted to reach the point of hermeneutics, but in doing so he destroyed a part of the text by demythologizing it.

For Perrin, the ultimate purpose of the entire process of interpretation was to "allow a text to speak, to make possible an appreciative reading of the text."[65] Literary criticism was a significant part of the process that enabled one to reach a "second naivete" with respect to the text (Ricoeur's term),[66] to "read" the text rather than "exegete" it (Funk's term),[67] to "appreciate" the text (Perrin's term). When this "hermeneutical moment" occurs "something happens" between the text and the reader.[68] Perrin

---

[63]Ibid., 12.

[64]Perrin, "Eschatology," 10.

[65]Perrin, *Language,* 203.

[66]Perrin referred to this term in *Language,* 155. Ricoeur used the term in "The Hermeneutics of Symbols and Philosophical Reflection," trans. Denis Savage, in Charles E. Reagan and David Steward, eds., *The Philosophy of Paul Ricoeur: An Anthology of His Work* (Boston: Beacon Press, 1978) 89. See also *Symbolism of Evil* where Ricoeur used the term throughout the book.

[67]Robert W. Funk, "The Good Samaritan as Methaphor," *Semeia* 2 (1974): 74-81.

[68]Perrin, "Literary Criticism," 370, 364.

considered this the "climax" of the hermeneutical process.[69] Textual, historical, and literary criticism were subordinate to hermenuetics and were designed to serve it.

Perrin's four-step program for interpreting a text is to be viewed as a combination of approaches which included the traditional historical-critical study of the Bible and biblical literary criticism stemming from the American New Critical movement. He did not make explicit reference to the American New Critical movement. It is evident, however, that his four-step program, which emphasized literary criticism, was indebted to and must be viewed against the background of the New Criticism. His concern for the form and language of a text was consistent with the New Critics' emphasis on what Ransom called the "precious object" itself. Like that of the New Critics, Perrin's approach led to a detailed analysis of literary features such as irony, paradox, metaphor, and movement. The form of a literary piece cannot be divorced from its meaning. All of these aspects of the theory and practice of criticism set forth in *Language* were primary concerns of the American New Criticism.

One other point is significant. From the beginning of the movement with *The Fugitives* magazine of poetry to the critical theory of Warren, Brooks, and others, the New Criticism has been primarily a criticism of poetry. The intensity of the New Criticism, the determination to unlock every word in a text, would be difficult if not impossible to sustain in a lengthy drama or a novel like *War and Peace*. Likewise, Perrin's literary criticism in *Language* was concerned with small units of the gospel tradition, namely the parables of Jesus and the symbol of the Kingdom of God. With respect to the symbol of the Kingdom of God, he drew upon the work of Wheelwright and Ricoeur, allies of the New Criticism. Wheelwright's investigation into the nature and kinds of symbols was used by Perrin to interpret and Kingdom of God.

It should be noted, however, that Perrin did have an interest in a literary criticism of the Gospel of Mark and, while his basic approach to that Gospel is available, his untimely death kept him from producing a full-length commentary on it. The point is that in his literary-critical work on Mark, he was at the same time utilizing the New Criticism and forging ahead of it by applying it to a unit of material much larger than a poem or parable.

Although Perrin used the New Criticism he was not a strict New Critic. His approach was a modification of the New Criticism along the same lines that can be observed in secular literary criticism. The first and second steps in his hermeneutical process constituted a historical analysis of a text. His concern for a historical understanding of a text is best understood from two perspectives. First, Perrin was incorporating into his approach methods he previously used. Form and redaction criticism were not dis-

---

[69]Perrin, *Language*, 12.

carded. Rather they, along with other historical concerns like date and authorship, were regarded as an essential first step in interpreting a text. Second, Perrin's incorporation of a historical concern into his approach paralleled a similar development in secular literary criticism exemplified by Wellek's and Warren's *Theory of Literature* and Krieger's *Window to Criticism.*

Paying attention to textual criticism, historical criticism, literary criticism, and hermeneutics is a way of maintaining a creative tension between the original meaning of a text and its contemporary relevance. Leander E. Keck, while recognizing the legitimacy of new approaches, cautioned against viewing any single method as a "meta-method": "There is little gain in replacing the tyranny of historical criticism with an equally imperious stance on the part of literary criticism."[70] Perrin's work in *Language* was, with respect to method, different from his earlier work. However, by building on his previous work he guarded against "replacing the tyranny of historical criticism" with some new "meta-method." The shift in *Language* was one of emphasis on a literary-critical interpretation of texts rather than on a historical interpretation.

Although Perrin's approach in *Language* must be set against the broad background of the New Criticism, he appropriated the New Critical approach through the work of New Testament literary critics, especially that of Wilder, Funk, Via, and Crossan, four scholars whose work Perrin discussed at some length in *Language.* His response to these four critics were essentially twofold: an appropriation of their modifications of the New Criticism, and an attempt to construct a holistic approach to the text which incorporated a concern for the historical context of a text into his hermeneutical program. Like Wilder, Funk, and Via, Perrin drew on the new hermeneutic to elucidate the encounter between text and reader. His contribution to this discussion was his arrangement of the process of interpretation into four steps. Via offered an exegesis of a number of Jesus' parables under the rubrics of historico-literary criticism, literary-existential analysis, and existential-theological interpretation, but provided no theoretical discussion of these rubrics. Perrin's four-step process, then, can be viewed as a clarification and refinement of Via's three steps.

• History and Literature •

The rise of literary criticism as a method in New Testament scholarship is difficult to categorize in terms of its position concerning the significance of the historical Jesus for faith. The reason for the difficulty is that literary criticism did not ask the question, "How significant is the historical Jesus for faith?" Rather, literary criticism asked, "How should

---

[70]Leander E. Keck, "Will the Historical-Critical Method Survive? Some Observations," in Richard A. Spencer, ed., *Orientation by Disorientation: Studies in Literary Criticism and Biblical Literary Criticism* (Pittsburg: Pickwick Press, 1980) 123.

a text be read?" Literary criticism centered the problem around the issue of hermeneutics rather than the issue of Christology.

One factor contributing to the rise of literary criticism among biblical scholars was the revolt against a nineteenth-century form of historicism which held that "what actually happened" with Jesus was what was significant. Since the historical-critical method was pressed into service to determine what actually happened, a revolt against historicism resulted to some degree in a revolt against historical criticism and a corresponding tendency toward a method that was unconcerned about what actually happened. I have already noted the same tendency in the New Criticism which was in part a revolt against the genetic fallacy of the older historical criticism. In New Testament scholarship, form and redaction criticism, while still historical methods, exhibit less of a interest in the historical Jesus than the nineteenth-century quest based on source-critical findings.

Given the literary-critical interest in the interpretation of a text or hermeneutics rather than an interest in the historical Jesus, it is not surprising to find that biblical literary critics drew on the "new hermeneutic" movement. The new hermeneutic of Fuchs and Ebeling was concerned with the faith that came to expression in Jesus as language event. Of the biblical literary critics surveyed earlier, Dan O. Via, Amos Wilder, and Robert W. Funk made explicit references to the new hermeneutic and the latter two contributed articles to *The New Hermeneutic*, an important discusson of the movement edited by James M. Robinson and John B. Cobb, Jr.

The important point for them seemed to be that through a literary analysis one encountered the "word" of the parable or story. It was the latter part, the encountering of the word in language, that was a continuation of the new hermeneutic emphasis. As Robert W. Funk wrote,

> But that to which one is ultimately attending, i.e., God's word to man, never draws near except as word event (Ebeling), so that there is no escape from the linguistic character of the kerygma. The incarnation is itself word event. *What* one is hearing in and through language and and the *hearing* are inextricably bound up together. Proclamation may be defined as the occurring word of God, i.e., word of God as word event. As such it is dependent upon a fresh *hearing* of the word. The relation between text and interpreter needs now to be opened up from the side of the interpreter, i.e., from the side of the hearing through which the text comes to expression as proclamation.[71]

The biblical literary critics, while they benefited from the new hermeneutic emphasis on the word in language, did not feel that enough attention was paid to the literary features of language in the new hermeneutic. Wilder, for example, said the new hermeneutic had "too

---

[71]Robert W. Funk, "The Hermeneutical Problem and Literary Criticism," in John B. Cobb, Jr., and James M. Robinson, eds., *The New Hermeneutic* (New York: Harper and Row, 1964) 172, 188.

much the character of an inner-theological pursuit" and that it should have paid more attention to anthropologists and literary critics who were making discoveries about the mythical and symbolic nature of language.[72]

The problem, even with literary criticism, can be understood as a problem of faith and history. However, for literary critics it was clearly not the problem of faith and the historical Jesus in particular, but rather the problem of faith and the historical text. The question was, "How much attention should be given to the historical context of a text when one interprets that text from, to, and for faith?" As already indicated the biblical literary critics, while they did not deny historical referents, did move interpretation to some degree away from a historical orientation. The focus was on the existential appropriation of the word of the text now rather than on what the text meant then.

As suggested earlier, Perrin's acceptance of redaction criticism was motivated in part by his developing view that it was the kerygma and not the historical Jesus that was significant for faith. The practice of redaction criticism further convinced him of the difficulty of gaining knowledge of the historical Jesus, given the theological nature of the sources. It also further convinced him of the inappropriateness of looking to the historical Jesus to support faith since the gospels were concerned with presenting the risen Lord of faith and not the earthly Jesus. Since it was both difficult and inappropriate to seek the basis of faith in history, he looked elsewhere for a foundation for faith. He was led to a reliance upon literary criticism, a method that allowed him to continue being a New Testament scholar while moving toward an ahistorical approach to meaning. He found meaning in the text itself and not primarily in its historical referents. He called this approach the hermeneutical process and discussed it in *Language*.

Perrin's approach in *Language*, which placed emphasis on the ahistorical features of a text, was a consistent and logical movement along the continuum I have described. It did lessen the problems associated with a more "conservative" view that bases faith on history. However, a movement toward the left side of the continuum opens up a new problem that can be stated in the form of a question: What are the controls on the interpretation of a literary text if the historical context is negated? To emphasize the "hermeneutical moment" at the expense of historical moorings may lead to subjective interpretations in which no degree of consensus is possible. One of the most articulate statements of this criticism is the book, *Validity in Interpretation*, by E. D. Hirsch, Jr. Hirsch argued that semantic autonomy or the view that a text has a life of its own

undercuts all criticism, even the sort which emphasizes present relevance.

---

[72]Amos N. Wilder, "The Word as Address and the Word as Meaning," in *New Hermeneutic*, 215-16.

If the view were correct, criticism would not only lack permanent validity, but could not even claim current validity by the time it got into print. Both the text's meaning and the tenor of the age would have altered. The "life" theory thus really masks the idea that the reader construes his own, new meaning instead of that represented by the text. . . . The "life" theory thus implicitly places the principle of change squarely where it belongs, that is, not in textual meaning as such, but in changing generations of readers.[73]

Many interpreters control the interpretation of a text by asking "what it meant and what it means."[74] The first question (what *did* the text mean), sometimes referred to as exegesis, can provide parameters for answering the second question (what *does* the text mean), sometimes referred to as exposition.[75] Hirsch was arguing that the movement away from a historical approach and toward a view that elevated the semantic autonomy of a text ignored the first question, thereby undercutting the validity of any answer to the second question. The historical-critical approach of most modern biblical studies has made great strides in determining what the various texts of the Bible meant. The question being addressed at this point is to what degree is Perrin's four-step hermeneutical program (which emphasized literary criticism) open to the criticism of Hirsch and others? In other words, what is the relationship of Perrin's approach as set forth in *Language*, to the historical-critical approach of most modern biblical studies?

Perrin abandoned the term "historical criticism" and substituted "hermeneutical process" to refer to his general approach to a biblical text. In his theoretical formulation of the hermeneutical process, he carefully protected his approach from the kind of criticism made by Hirsch by including what he called textual and historical criticism in the four-step approach. Two observations can be made at this point. First, Perrin provided in *Language* very little exegetical work. It is, therefore, difficult to know how susceptible his hermeneutical program is to the problem to which Hirsch referred. Second, while he advocated the integration of historical and ahistorical literary analysis, it is clear that his movement with respect to method was toward a more ahistorical approach which placed less and less emphasis on history. The approach in *Language* and the related issue of history and meaning can be set in some perspective by noting two other approaches being given increasing attention by biblical scholars.

Both structual criticism and canonical criticism, when strictly defined, can be viewed as approaching the Bible with an ahistorical bias. Struc-

---

[73]E. D. Hirsch, Jr., *Validity in Interpretation* (New Haven CT: Yale University Press, 1967) 213.

[74]Krister Stendahl used this phrase in "Biblical Theology, Contemporary," in *Interpreter's Dictionary of the Bible,* supp: 419.

[75]Notice the format of the well-known *Interpreter's Bible Commentary* (Nashville: Abingdon Press).

turalism is the form of literary criticism that is the most radical in its denigration of history. Structural critics attempt to investigate the deep structures of a text, structures that are understood to be transtemporal and transpatial.[76] Many commentators agree that the philosophical question raised by the practice of structuralism is that of the significance of history.[77] Structuralism tends to divorce meaning from history and McKnight said that meaning for the "strict structuralist" is not related to history.[78] Utilizing Bultmann's term, Daniel Patte said the introduction of structural methods implies a shift in the critic's "preunderstanding" of the biblical text.[79] Patte contrasted literary or structural criticism to other methods. In form and redaction criticism, he noted

> The texts refer beyond themselves to events, situations, conflicts, ideas—and meaning is not really available apart from this reference. [But with literary criticism] the text is grasped as a whole or totality, as people read it, rather than as something to be analyzed (into traditions and redactions), and meaning is seen to be a functon not of the relationship between text and historical setting, but primarily of the union of form and content in the text itself.[80]

The literary criticism of Perrin was not strictly structuralist and he never entered to a substantial degree into the structuralist discussion. He did provide a brief negative evaluation of structural criticism in *Language*. That criticism, however, was limited to structuralism's value for parable interpretation. Perrin did not feel this method of criticism did justice to the literary features of the parables of Jesus. However, he held out the possiblity that structural criticism might be very helpful in interpreting other biblical texts.[81] Although Perrin cannot be called a structural critic, structuralism is an example of the kind of approach that helps bring into focus the direction in which his literary criticism seemed to be moving in *Language*. Via is an example of a scholar whose work moved from literary

---

[76]See Daniel Patte, *What is Structural Exegesis?* Guides to Biblical Scholarship, ed. Dan O. Via, Jr. (Philadelphia: Fortress Press, 1976) 1.

[77]For example, Robert A. Spivey, in "Structuralism and Biblical Studies: The Uninvited Guest," *Interpretation* 28 (April 1974): 143, said the basic issue raised by structural criticism is that of the "relationship of structure of history." In his evaluation of structuralism as a method for biblical studies, Edgar V. McKnight, in "Structure and Meaning in Biblical Narrative," *Perspectives in Religious Studies* 3 (Spring 1976): 13, observed that "The value of structuralism for interpretation is related to the prior evaluation of the importance of history for meaning."

[78]McKnight "Structure and Meaning," 13.

[79]Patte, *Structural Exegesis*, 1.

[80]Ibid., iii-iv. It should be added, however, that Patte himself advocates utilizing both structuralism and traditional historical criticism.

[81]Perrin, *Language*, 204-205.

criticism into structural criticism. Via's early book, *Parables*, was a literary-critical discussion of the parables; a later work, *Kerygma and Comedy in the New Testament: A Structuralist Approach to Hermeneutic*[82] was, as indicated by the title, an attempt at structural criticism.

Canonical criticism also directs the critical focus to the final, and in this case canonical, form of a biblical book and to the continuing historical referents in the life and history of the believing community. In doing so, it affirms that the text's significance is not found in its original historical referents.[83]

In summary, structual criticism, canonical criticism, and a strictly defined literary criticism, while approaching the text from different perspectives, all have a tendency to view it as, to use Krieger's metaphor, a mirror that locks meaning in. In *Language* Perrin moved toward a much greater appreciation of this mirror-like quality of a text while maintaining, theoretically at least, the window-like quality of a text as well.

---

[82]Via, *Parables* (1967); *Kerygma and Comedy in the New Testament: A Structuralist Approach to Hermeneutic* (Philadelphia: Fortress Press, 1975).

[83]The best example of a canonical-critical approach to the Bible is Brevard S. Childs, *Introduction to the Old Testament as Scripture* (Philadelphia: Fortress Press, 1979). For a discussion of the problem of history in Childs's approach, see John Priest, "Canon and Criticism: A Review Article," *Journal of the American Academy of Religion* 48 (June 1980): 259-71; and Ralph W. Klein, Gary Stansell, and Walter Brueggemann, "The Childs' Proposal: A Symposium," *Word & World* 1 (Spring 1981): 105-15.

·PART II·

RETHINKING THE TEACHING OF JESUS

THE TEACHING:
THE KINGDOM OF GOD

• The Continental Discussion •

In the scholarly discusson of the Kingdom of God and, as we will see later, the parables, one finds a tension between their historical context and meaning in life of Jesus and their continuing relevance. Some scholars concerned themselves primarily with the historical context and meaning while others focused on the contemporary impact and relevance of the teaching of Jesus. Still other attempts were made to maintain a viable connection between the two.

As interest in Life of Jesus research declined toward the end of the nineteenth century, attention became focused on the teaching of Jesus, and especially on the Kingdom of God, a dominant theme of that teaching. Since the nineteenth century every major interpreter of the Kingdom of God in Jesus' teaching has agreed that the Kingdom is the main theme of Jesus' proclamation. The term "Kingdom of God" (ἡ βασιλεία τοῦ θεοῦ) or an equivalent expression[1] is found frequently in Jesus' teaching, occurring in Mark, Q, and the special sources of Matthew and Luke—M and L. As the following survey will show, however, interpreters have not agreed about the nature, meaning, and continuing relevance of the Kingdom of God.

In scholarly circles the issue of the Kingdom of God was raised to the center of theological discussion by nineteenth-century liberal theologians. These theologians, such as Albrecht Ritschl[2] and Adolf von Har-

---

[1]Such as ἡ βασιλεία τῶν οὐρανῶν or simply ἡ βασιλεία.

[2]See, for example, Albrecht Ritschl, *The Christian Doctrine of Justification and Reconciliation*, 2nd ed., trans. A. B. Macaulay, ed H. R. Mackintosh (Edinburgh: T. and T. Clark, 1902 [1847]). Another good statement of Ritschl's position on the Kingdom of God is the popular little book, *Instruction in the Christian Religion*, trans. Albert T. Swing. Included in Swing, *The Theology of Albrecht Ritschl* (London: Longmans, Green, 1901).

nack,[3] were, however, primarily interested in employing the Kingdom of God concept to set forth an ethic relevant for their own time. They made little attempt to offer careful exegesis of Jesus' teaching or to set it against its historical background. These liberal theologians in effect ignored any supernatural notion of the Kingdom of God in the teaching of Jesus, emphasizing rather its present tense and individualistic nature as expressed in love. Jesus became, then, the religious personality par excellence, the one who fulfilled the ideal humanity.

As theologians primarily concerned with a relevant ethic, these liberal scholars did not provide exegetical studies. They did, however, often cite texts from the gospels to support their notion of the Kingdom of God. One of their favorite texts was Luke 17:20-21.

> Being asked by the Pharisees when the kingdom of God was coming, he answered the, "The kingdom of God is not coming with signs to be observed; nor will they say, 'Lo, here it is!' or 'There!' for behold, the kingdom of God is in the midst of you (ἐντὸς ὑμῶν)."

The meaning of this saying depends on how the problematic Greek expression ἐντὸς ὑμῶν is translated. The two possiblities are "within you" and "in the midst of you." The liberal scholars of the nineteenth century preferred the former and viewed the saying as referring to the rule of God in the hearts of men, obviously because it supported their notion of the Kingdom of God.

The first serious blow to the prevailing liberal interpretations of the Kingdom of God in Jesus' teaching was Johannes Weiss's *Jesus' Proclamation of the Kingdom of God.*[4] Exhibiting a concern for the proclamation of the historical Jesus, he insisted that Jesus' teaching about the Kingdom of God must be viewed against the background of apocalyptic Judaism which made a sharp distinction between the world above and the world below. In such a dualistic framework, the Kingdom of God was associated with the world above in opposition to the world below which was ruled by Satan. This Jewish apocalyptic framework was the criterion that determined what he viewed as authentic in the teaching of Jesus.

Weiss said Jesus expected this superworldly Kingdom in the future and that his ethic was ascetical and emphasized repentance as preparation for one's entrance into the coming Kingdom. Repentance meant turning from the present world and seeking, above all else, God and the imminent Kingdom. Sayings such as Mark 1:15, Matthew 10:7, and Luke 10:9, which refer to the Kingdom as "at hand" (ἤγγικεν), were used by Weiss to support his futuristic interpretation and to control the interpretation of say-

---

[3]See, for example, Adolf von Harnack, *What is Christianity?* 3rd ed., trans. Thomas Bailey Saunders (New York: G. P. Putnam's Sons, 1912).

[4]Johannes Weiss, *Jesus' Proclamation of the Kingdom of God,* trans. and ed. Richard H. Hiers and David L. Holland (Philadelphia: Fortress Press, 1971).

ings such as Matthew 12:28 ‖ Luke 11:20 that say the Kingdom "has come" (ἔφθασεν).

Albert Schweitzer developed the approach of Weiss into a "thorough-going eschatology" *(konsequente Eschatologie)* which included the entire life and work of Jesus as well as his teaching.[5] Paying particular attention to Jesus' ethic, he coined the phrase "interim ethic" *(Interimsethik)*. It was an interim ethic because it was in force only for the time between the proclamation of the Kingdom of God its imminent coming. The ethic had to do with repentance or moral renewal as a preparation for the coming Kingdom.[6] Jesus did not provide ethical instruction for his disciples that was to be normative for all human conduct. Because the time was short, the ethic of Jesus was a special one, designed only for the interim before the end.[7]

Schweitzer took his theory a step further by emphasizing the significance of the Mission of the Twelve in Matthew 10. The sending was Jesus' last effort to bring in the Kingdom of God. Since the parousia did not come as he expected, Jesus, according to Schweitzer, altered his plans and attempted to force its coming with his own death. Since that too failed, he died a disillusioned figure.

Unlike the nineteenth-century liberal interpretations the apocalyptic and futuristic interpretations of Weiss and Schweitzer raise the possibility of a tension between the historical Jesus' proclamation of the Kingdom of God and its continuing relevance. Neither Weiss nor Schweitzer viewed the apocalyptic proclamation of Jesus as having ongoing relevance. Subsequent scholarship, while generally accepting the contention that Jesus' teaching had an apocalyptic and futuristic orientation, often attempted to interpret that proclamation in such a way that it could be relevant in contemporary life.

The theological program of Rudolf Bultmann has been by far the most influential attempt to do justice to the nature of Jesus' proclamation while at the same time interpreting the proclamation so that it has continuing relevance. Bultmann accepted the general conclusion of Weiss and

---

[5]For Schweitzer's views, see *The Mystery of the Kingdom of God: The Secret of Jesus; Messiahship and Passion,* trans. Walter Lowrie (New York: Macmillan, 1950 [1901]); and *The Quest of the Historical Jesus: A Critical Study of Its Progress from Reimarus to Wrede,* trans. W. Montgomery (New York: Macmillan, 1968 [1906]).

[6]Schweitzer, *Mystery of the Kingdom,* 53.

[7]It should be noted, however, that Schweitzer also saw Jesus as having a world-affirming ethic of love and service that contradicted his world-negating apocalyptic preaching and interim ethic. It was this inconsistency in Jesus that attracted Schweitzer. Subsequent scholarship generally has paid very little attention to this aspect of Schweitzer's interpretation. For a discussion of it, see Jackson Lee Ice, *Schweitzer: Prophet of Radical Theology* (Philadelphia: Westminster Press, 1971) 153-74, esp. 156-58, 161-63.

Schweitzer that the Kingdom of God was an apocalyptic concept and that Jesus expected its arrival in the near future. Since humankind today does not accept the world view presupposed by apocalypticism, how can the Kingdom of God be made relevant? Bultmann's answer was that the first-century mythological Jewish notions should be reinterpreted with the central idea expressed in categories that are relevant today. He drew these categories from the philosophy of Martin Heidegger and interpreted the imminent future in Jesus' message existentially. The essential point is that the imminent future confronts human beings who stand at the moment of decision. The Kingdom of God, then, while entirely in the future, is made present in the sense that it forces us to a decision now.

Given his existentialist perspective, Bultmann could, unlike Weiss and Schweitzer, maintain a kind of continuity between Jesus' proclamation and an ethic that had continuing relevance. He rejected any kind of temporary or interim ethic and argued that the radical ethical demand of Jesus, like his proclamation of the Kingdom, brings one to the moment of decision. Jesus' eschatological message and his ethical message are a unity.[8]

The "realized eschatology" of C. H. Dodd was another influential and creative approach to the problem of the relationship between Jesus' proclamation and its continuing relevance. Unlike Bultmann, Dodd said that the Kingdom of God was a present entity (that is, "realized") in Jesus' own ministry. He argued that the sayings of Jesus that declare that the Kingdom of God has already come are explicit and the sayings that imply a future coming of the Kingdom must be interpreted from the perspective of "realized eschatology."[9] This program of interpretation gave him a base from which to deny any kind of interim ethic and to see Jesus' proclamation as having continuing relevance. Although the message of the historical Jesus was his main concern, at least explicitly, Dodd suggested that "realized eschatology" had relevance for subsequent Christian faith in general and the sacramental life of the church in particular.[10]

A third attempt to find a relevant ethic in Jesus' teaching, different from that of Bultmann, who acknowledged the futuristic perspective of Jesus, and Dodd, who acknowledged only a present tense perspective, was made be W. G. Kümmel in *Promise and Fulfilment*. Following an examination of the important sayings, he concluded that both future-oriented

---

[8]See Rudolf Bultmann, *Theology of the New Testament*, 2 vols. (New York: Charles Scribner's Sons, 1951-1955) 1:20-21.

[9]For Dodd, this meant that most of the sayings that speak about a future coming have their origin in the later church rather than in the historical Jesus. Dodd saw some sayings that imply a future Kingdom as referring to the continuation of Jesus' work and to a Kingdom so close that Jesus saw it as one eschatological event that was in progress.

[10]See C. H. Dodd, *The Parables of the Kingdom*, rev. ed. (New York: Charles Scribner's Sons, 1961 [1935]) 163ff.

sayings and present-oriented sayings stood side-by-side in Jesus' proclamation. Because Jesus spoke of a present Kingdom, Kümmel argued that his eschatological message could not be labeled as apocalyptic, which looked for salvation only in the future. Jesus' proclamation was an eschatological message designed to prepare persons now for the future, not an apocalyptic revelation of specific future events.[11]

Perrin's first discussion of the Kingdom of God in Jesus' teaching came in *Kingdom of God*.[12] There he accepted the consensus of scholarship that the Kingdom of God was an apocalyptic concept in Jesus' proclamation. He added, however, that the meaning and use of the Kingdom of God as an apocalyptic concept was not a matter of consenus. It was at this point that he set forth his own view.

Perrin began with a discussion of the concepts of history and the end-time in the Old Testament and argued that prophetic eschatology was the true background for Jewish apocalyptic and for the Kingdom of God in Jesus' proclamation. For Perrin the essential element in prophetic eschatology was the future activity of God on behalf of the people. Apocalyptic eschatology still looked for the prophetic eschatological event; that event, however, became expressed in new forms. The coming event would bring in an age wholly new and different from the present age. The new forms of expression involved a manifold variety of images and descriptions related to the new age, figures appearing at the end-time, and events connected with the end-time. Perrin's particular contribution to this discussion was his insistence that

> this bewildering complex of [Jewish apocalyptic] expectation does, in fact, revolve around two central themes: God's decisive intervention in history and human experience, and the final state of the redeemed to which the intervention leads.[13]

In terms of the decisive intervention of God, Perrin contended that Jesus rejected the apocalyptic conception of history which focused on a preordained climax, and returned to a prophetic understanding which focused on God's activity in the eschatological event and the challenge of persons in that activity. He supported this contention with exegeses of sayings such a Mark 1:15 and Luke 17:20-21. In a brief exegesis of the first saying, which reads, "The time is fulfilled, and the Kingdom of God is at

---

[11]W. G. Kümmel, *Promise and Fulfillment: The Eschatological Message of Jesus*, 3rd ed., trans. Dorothea M. Barton (Naperville IL: Alec R. Allenson, 1957 [1956]) 141.

[12]Norman Perrin, *The Kingdom of God in the Teaching of Jesus* (Philadelphia: Westminster Press, 1963). *Kingdom of God* was, for the most part, a history of the scholarly discussion. Perrin's summary of the discussion and tentative answers to points still unresolved came in the last chapter.

[13]This paragraph summarizes Perrin, *Kingdom of God*, 162-68; the quotation is from 167.

hand; repent, and believe the gospel," he stated that the people were challenged by the proclamation that God's decisive intervention was at hand.[14] The second saying reads,

> Being asked by the Pharisees when the Kingdom of God was coming, he answered them, "The kingdom of God in not coming with signs to be observed; nor will they say, 'Lo, here it is!' or 'There!' for behold, the kingdom of God is in the midst of you (ἐντὸς ὑμῶν)."

Here Perrin, like the liberal scholars, Dodd, and others,[15] interpreted Jesus as rejecting the apocalyptic view of history which calculated the coming of the Kingdom in advance and looked for signs related to its coming.[16]

At this point Perrin made more explicit the important distinction between prophetic and apocalyptic eschatology crucial for his exegesis.

> The prophets had anchored their hopes for the future in the certainty that God had acted in certain historical events, was acting and would act. This activity was a challenge to Israel to repent. . . . In all this it was not the history in itself that was important but the fact that God was active in it, that he was entering into it and challenging them within it. The important thing about history, for apocalyptic, is that it is running a predetermined course to a predetermined climax, all in accordance with the divine plan . . . the individual events have ceased to be important as events in which God is active and through which he may be known.[17]

Jesus proclaimed the final and decisive activity of God in redeeming the people without implying that this activity must occur in any specific form.

Perrin found further support for his view in Jesus' choice of "Kingdom of God." This expression emphasized the kingly activity of God as opposed to apocalyptic expressions such as "the consummation" or "the end of days," which emphasized the end. In Jewish apocalyptic, the phrase "Kingdom of God" occurred only five times with respect to the divine intervention of God.[18] Even the teaching of Jesus which lies behind the synoptic apocalypses[19]

> puts the emphasis upon the sudden and unexpected manner of God's inbreaking into history and human experience and upon the responsibility

---

[14]Perrin, *Kingdom of God*, 170-71.

[15]See Richard H. Hiers, *The Kingdom of God in the Synoptic Tradition* (Gainesville: University of Florida Press, 1970) 22ff., for a discussion of the interpretation of Luke 17:20-21 by various scholars.

[16]Perrin, *Kingdom of God*, 175.

[17]Ibid., 176-77.

[18]Ps Sol 17:3; Sib Orac 3:46-47; Test Mos 10:1; 1QM 6:6; and 1QM 12:7.

[19]Probably preserved in Luke 17:22-37, 21:34-36, and Mark 13:32-37, according to Perrin, who accepted T. W. Manson's conclusions about what is authentic here.

of men to be prepared to respond to the crisis, thus reiterating the prophetic rather than the apocalyptic emphases.[20]

With regard to the final state of the redeemed, Perrin found only two certain instances[21] of the term "Kingdom of God" in Jewish apocalyptic. In the teaching of Jesus this usage was common, as for example in the Beatitudes. Perrin concluded that the term "Kingdom of God" was rare in Jewish apocalyptic, but that it did occur in reference to God's intervention and the final state of the redeemed.

> In precisely these same ways it is used in the teaching of Jesus, with the significant difference that what is rare in apocalyptic is normative in the teaching of Jesus. This difference indicates a difference in emphasis and a difference in the understanding of history. By his use of the term Jesus puts all emphasis upon the activity of God, and he implies that history is the sphere in which the activity is manifest . . . the one emphasis is upon the activity of God as decisive for man's salvation and as securing for man the perfect relationship with God envisaged in the imagery of the perfect state.[22]

In his interpretation of the time of the Kingdom of God, Perrin agreed with Manson, Jeremias, Kümmel, and others that it is both present and future in Jesus' proclamation. Although Jesus did look toward a consummation in the future, Perrin stressed that he did not offer any detailed instruction as to its nature or exact time. Again, Perrin's emphasis was on the activity of God in events and the response of people to that activity.

Perrin's understanding of the relationship between Jesus' eschatology and ethics followed from his prophetic interpretation of the Kingdom of God. "The ultimate purpose of the intervention of God in history and human experience," Perrin wrote, "is to make it possible for man to enter a new and perfect relationship with himself." The design of ethical teaching, Perrin added, is "to illustrate the kind of response which man must make in order to enter into this relationship."[23] Although he explicitly accepted Weiss and Schweitzer's insistence that the Kingdom of God must be understood in terms of apocalyptic, Perrin's discussion of the meaning and use of Kingdom of God actually negated this acceptance. His concern was to identify Jesus with a prophetic eschatology that had a positive view of history and saw history as the arena of God's revelation and activity. Apocalyptic ideas negate history and emphasize a wholly new order. This fact explains why Perrin turned to Gerhard von Rad for his understanding of the Kingdom of God in the Old Testament.

---

[20]Perrin, *Kingdom of God*, 178.

[21]Sib Orac 3:767-71 and 1QSb 4:25-26.

[22]Perrin, *Kingdom of God*, 178-85; the quotation is found on 184-85.

[23]Ibid., 201.

Von Rad's work was based upon his view that history was an essential category in Old Testament revelation.[24]

Perrin's attempt to relate the Kingdom of God in Jesus' teaching to prophetic eschatology was consistent with and supported the position concerning the relationship between faith and history that he held when he wrote *Kingdom of God*. I have shown that early in his career he emphasized the importance of the historical Jesus for faith. Although Perrin did not discuss this issue, it seems difficult to understand how a historical Jesus who looked for the intervention of God that would end history and establish a wholly new order (apocalyptic eschatology) can have continuing relevance, especially when that scenario did not occur. A Jesus who saw the historical as the sphere of God's working and did not set an exact time for the coming new age (prophetic eschatology) can much more easily be interpreted as having continuing relevance.

The difficulty associated with accepting Jesus as an apocalyptic preacher and utilizing him as a source for a relevant ethic, a difficulty that, as I have suggested, lay behind Perrin's work in *Kingdom of God*, was not a new one. The nineteenth-century liberals sidestepped the difficulty by interpreting the apocalyptic elements as the husk of Jesus' teaching and not its true kernel. Weiss and Schweitzer, in accepting the apocalyptic nature of Jesus' proclamation, were left with no relevent ethic originating directly from Jesus' teaching. Dodd and Kümmel denied the apocalypticism in Jesus while Bultmann radically reinterpreted it. Although his specific formulation was different, Perrin, like the liberal theologians, Dodd, and Kümmel, in effect denied the apocalyptic and radically futuristic nature of Jesus' teaching in order to find in that teaching ongoing relevance. Richard H. Hiers, who identifies his own position as in the tradition of Weiss and Schweitzer, also makes this criticism, charging that most scholars have failed to accept fully the apocalyptic nature of Jesus' teaching because they could not reconcile that acceptance with their faith. Although he did not discuss Perrin's work, his criticism, as we have suggested, is valid for Perrin's interpretation in *Kingdom of God*.[25]

Perrin's theologically motivated interest in the historical Jesus led him to engage more directly and intensely in an attempt to "rediscover" Je-

---

[24]For example, Gerhard von Rad, *Old Testament Theology*, 2 vols., trans. D. M. G. Stalker (New York: Harper and Row, 1962 [1957], 1965 [1960]) 1:106.

[25]Richard H. Hiers, *The Historical Jesus and the Kingdom of God*, University of Florida Humanities Monograph Series 38 (Gainesville: University of Florida Press, 1973) 1ff. See also his book, *The Kingdom of God in the Synoptic Tradition*. It should be noted, however, that with the discoveries at Nag Hammadi increasing doubts are being raised as to the apocalyptic genesis of early Christianity. See Helmut Koester, *History and Literature of Early Christianity*, vol. 2 of *Introduction to the New Testament* (Philadelphia: Fortress Press, 1982) 150-54, where he discusses the Gospel of Thomas, emphasizing its presentation of Jesus as a teacher of wisdom.

sus' teaching about the Kingdom of God. That attempt came in his next major study, *Rediscovering*. By that time he had come fully under the influence of Bultmann and had entered into his own form-critical study of the gospels. In *Kingdom of God* he assumed the authenticity of certain sayings form critics had traced back to Jesus and concentrated on the meaning of the Kingdom of God in light of those sayings. In *Rediscovering* he entered fully into the form-critical discussion of the Kingdom of God as a theme of the historical Jesus in addition to continuing his discussion of the meaning of authentic Kingdom sayings.

As a form critic, Perrin's particular contribution to the study of the Kingdom of God was his application of the criterion of dissimilarity to the Kingdom of God in order to provide specific evidence for its authenticity. He began by developing three ways in which the Kingdom of God in Jesus' teaching differed from both Judaism and the early church. First, Jesus' teaching differed in that it used the expression "Kingdom of God" to refer to the final act of God in visiting and redeeming the people. In this usage no particular form of the act of God is implied and no particular accompanying phenomena must be present. The Jewish eschatological hope in Jesus' day differed in that it generally associated all kinds of pictures and ideas with this final act of God. This difference was especially true for the apocalyptic literature. This first usage of Kingdom of God is not found in the New Testament outside the synoptic gospels.

Second, "Kingdom of God" in the synoptic gospels is a comprehensive term for the blessings of salvation. In the Judaism of Jesus' day the dominant term used to express the blessings of salvation was the "age to come." Only in a few instances was "Kingdom of God" used as a comprehensive term for the blessings of salvation in the New Testament (outside the synoptic gospels). Perrin showed that the few times that "Kingdom of God" was used in this way were dissimilar in other ways to the synoptic tradition.

Third, the expression "Kingdom of God" was used in the synoptic gospels to speak of the Kingdom of God as "coming." In Jewish texts the Kingdom was usually "established," as in the Kaddish prayer. In Jesus' teaching the Kingdom was never spoken of as "established." In the early church, it was Jesus who was to come and not the Kingdom of God. These three points constituted what Perrin called "fundamental emphases" in Jesus' Kingdom proclamation.[26]

With these points established by the criterion of dissimilarity, Perrin moved on to evaluate specific sayings. He stood with most form critics in

---

[26]Norman Perrin,*Rediscovering the Teaching of Jesus* (New York: Harper and Row, 1976 [1967]) 54-63. Perrin discussed the first two points in *Kingdom of God*. In *Rediscovering*, however, he supported the argument for authenticity by giving special atttention to the way they are dissimilar both to the Judaism of Jesus' day and to the early church.

accepting as authentic Luke 11:20: "But if it is by the finger of God that I cast out demons then the Kingdom of God has come upon you." It satisfies the criterion of dissimilarity because of its reference to eschatological activity of God and because of its notion that the Kingdom "comes." As to its meaning, Perrin suggested that the saying interprets the exorcisms. According to him, the thrust of the saying is that the exorcisms are an experience of the Kingdom of God. In addition, the emphasis is on the individual and his experience of the Kingdom of God, rather than on the people of God as a whole.[27]

Luke 17:20-21, another saying with high claims to authenticity, speaks of the Kingdom in terms of God's decisive intervention in history and human experience, and it speaks of the Kingdom as "coming." As to the meaning of the saying, Perrin reiterated his belief, originally stated in *Kingdom of God* and unlike that of Weiss, that Luke 17:20-21 denies the apocalyptic concept of history which emphasized signs to be observed, and returns to a prophetic view of history. Unlike his previous interpretation, though, he suggested that Luke 17:20-21 modifies the prophetic view of history, which looked for God's activity in specific events, and, when viewed in light of Luke 11:20, emphasizes that God's activity is to be known in the experience of individuals. Although Perrin translated ἐντὸς ὑμῶν as "among you" rather than "within you," he interpreted the phrase to mean "in the experience of the individual."[28] His emphasis on the individual was probably the result of the increasing influence on his work of the existentialist approach taken by Bultmann.[29]

The third important Kingdom saying Perrin examined in *Rediscovering* was Matthew 11:12: "From the days of John the Baptist until now the kingdom of heaven has suffered violence, and men of violence take it by force." He considered this saying authentic in part because it reflects a high estimate of John and as such is characteristic of Jesus and not of the early church.[30] In this saying Jesus was affirming that John was the initiator of the new aeon that declared that "Now is the time of God's decisive activity!"[31] The second half of the saying affirms that the present aeon is a time of conflict. Whereas Luke 11:20 indicates victory, Matthew 11:12 suggests that the Kingdom of God can even suffer a measure of de-

---

[27]Ibid., 63-67.

[28]Ibid., 68-74.

[29]See *Kingdom of God*, 187, for Perrin's reference to Bultmann's influence.

[30]Perrin considered the parallel, Luke 16:16, to be secondary because it has Lukan characteristics such as the notion of an epoch ending with John and the phrase about preaching the good news of the Kingdom. In addition, the phrase "everyone enters it violently" smooths out Matthew's version at this point.

[31]This phrase is similar to one of Jeremias's categories for the parables, "Now is the Day of Salvation."

feat. As Perrin put it, "The outcome of the battle may be sure, but the casulties are going to be real, not sham."[32]

In summary, Perrin's study of the Kingdom of God in *Rediscovering* was, for the most part, a detailed reformulation of and argument for the conclusions he arrived at in *Kingdom of God*. The strength of his study in *Rediscovering*, and what made it different from that in *Kingdom of God*, was his application of the criteria of authenticity to the Kingdom of God sayings in order to firmly establish the proclamation of the historical Jesus. The major weakness of his study was his failure to discuss adequately the significance for faith of the authentic teaching he discovered. In *Rediscovering* he set forth a position whereby knowledge of the historical Jesus contributed to the formulation of one's faith-image. He did not complete the task by showing specifically how what he had learned about the Kingdom of God contributed to that faith-image. Even though he did not make explicit how Jesus' Kingdom of God teaching could contribute to the faith-image, it does seem clear that he believed it could.

• The American Reformulation •

Perrin's next major study of the Kingdom of God came in *Language*, which exhibits a decided literary turn in interpreting the Kingdom of God. There he began by tracing the development of the Kingdom in ancient Jewish literature.[33] The roots of the symbol Kingdom of God are found in the ancient Near Eastern myth of God acting as king in creating and renewing the earth. This myth, celebrated annually in cultic ritual and common to many ancient Near Eastern peoples, was adapted by the Hebrews and expressed in the enthronement psalms.[34] This tradition combined with a second tradition, that of Salvation History. The history of God's acts of salvation for the people was confessed in summary "credos."[35] The symbol Kingdom of God, then, evoked the myth of God who created the world (ancient Near Eastern myth) and was active on behalf of the people in that world (Salvation History). The symbol was dependent on the myth and was effective because it evoked the myth. The myth was effective because of its ability to interpret the experience of the people.

The symbol and myth effectively enabled the people to interpret their experience of exodus, conquest, and settlement. Even with the fall of the Northern kingdom in 721 B.C.E. and the Southern kingdom in 587 B.C.E., the myth was maintained by the prophets, who saw these events as God's redemptive judgment on the people. The Jews again lost their indepen-

---

[32]Perrin, *Rediscovering*, 74-77; the quotation is from 77.

[33]Norman Perrin, *Jesus and the Language of the Kingdom: Symbol and Metaphor in New Testament Interpretation* (Philadelphia: Fortress Press, 1976) 16-32.

[34]Pss 47, 93, 96, 97, 98, 99.

[35]For example, Deut 26:5b-10; 6:20-24.

dence in 63 B.C.E. The symbol and myth remained, but after 63 B.C.E. it expressed a hope. This apocalyptic tradition[36] simply reformulated the myth into more metaphorical imagery and looked for a dramatic irruption of God into history. Perrin's point was that the symbol evoked the myth of God active on behalf of the people, but that the expectation varied according to the particular circumstances of the people.

To support this notion of the "plurisignificant" nature of symbols, he drew on the "newer" New Criticism of Philip Wheelwright and Paul Ricoeur. Like Wheelwright, Ricoeur, and others, Perrin made a distinction between two different kinds of symbols and utilized "steno-symbol" and "tensive symbol," terms introduced by Wheelwright and discussed earlier. With this distinction in mind and utilizing Wheelwright's terms, he interpreted the symbol Kingdom of God in ancient Judaism as being fundamentally a tensive symbol whose meaning was not completely exhausted by any one referent. This became what Via, in a review of *Language*, called the "governing motif" in Perrin's discussion of Kingdom of God.[37] There were times, however, when Kingdom of God was used primarily as a steno-symbol. Ancient Jewish apocalyptic is a good example of this use because of its penchant for identifying historical individuals as the Messiah and looking for the intervention of God at a specific time.[38]

He used this distinction between kinds of symbols, a distinction derived from general literary criticism, to arrive at a historical understanding of Kingdom of God in the message of Jesus. He said the meaning of Kingdom of God on the lips of Jesus had been a difficult problem because scholars had generally started with the notion that Jesus had a "concept" of the Kingdom of God. They then asked what was this concept, or, to use Wheelwright's term, to what did the steno-symbol refer? Weiss and Schweitzer argued that it was an apocalyptic conception. Bultmann saw it as a conception of human existence. Dodd focused on the time of the Kingdom and interpreted Jesus' conception as including both a present and future aspect. But to presuppose the Kingdom of God was a steno-symbol on the lips of Jesus was to imply that he had a constant and well-defined understanding of how God's activity would be manifest and to set limits on the results of the investigation.

Perrin interpreted a number of the Kingdom sayings in light of his new understanding of symbol. Luke 17:20-21 was interpreted in some detail in *Kingdom of God*, *Rediscovering*, and *Language*. The concern of this saying is to deny an incorrect understanding of the proclamation. In *Kingdom of*

---

[36]For example, Test Mos 10.

[37]Dan O. Via, Review of *Jesus and the Language*, in *Interpretation* 31 (January 1977): 181.

[38]Perrin, *Language*, 31-32.

God[39] he interpreted this saying as denying apocalyptic history which viewed all of history as running a predetermined course in accordance with the divine plan. Jesus was affirming the prophetic view of history that emphasized knowing God through activity in specific events. In *Rediscovering* he still viewed the saying as denying the apocalyptic concept. He also saw it as modifying the prophetic view of history because God's activity in specific events is ἐντὸς ὑμῶν, translated "among you," but interpreted as meaning "in the experience of the individual," and not in such a way that one could say "Lo,here!" or "Lo,there!"[40] In *Language* he interpreted the saying in terms of symbol and myth.

> Jesus categorically rejected the seeking after "signs to be observed" and in so doing necessarily equally categorically rejected the treatment of the myth as allegory and its symbols as steno-symbols. In the message of Jesus the myth is true myth and the symbols of God's redemptive activity are tensive symbols.[41]

In *Kingdom of God* Perrin interpreted the saying as referring to the activity of God in specific events and in *Rediscovering* to the activity of God in the experience of the individual. In his latest consideration of this saying, he adopted a much open-ended interpretation, seeing the Kingdom of God as a tensive symbol which could evoke a whole set of meanings.

Again, in the case of Luke 11:20, Perrin combined his previous interpretations into a new perspective. Dodd and others had viewed this saying as support for the Kingdom as a present conception, Perrin noted, "But these are not the right terms in which to discuss it." Perrin preferred to "recognize that Jesus is deliberately evoking the myth of the activity of God on behalf of his people, and claiming that the exorcisms are a manifestation of that activity in the experience of his hearer." This recognition, Perrin concluded,

> establishes the fact that Kingdom of God is not a steno- but a tensive symbol on the lips of Jesus. Clearly the exorcisms do not exhaust the possibilities with regard to the activity of God on behalf of his people; the meaning of the symbol is not exhausted by any one apprehension of the reality if represents.[42]

Matthew 11:12 was interpreted as evoking the myth of God engaged in eschatological conflict with evil, a variation of the myth of God active as king. In *Rediscovering* the emphasis of his interpretation was on the authenticity of the saying and on Jesus' understanding of John the Baptist.

---

[39]Perrin, *Kingdom of God*, 176-78.

[40]Perrin, *Rediscovering*, 72-74.

[41]Perrin, *Language*, 45.

[42]Ibid., 43.

He emphasized that Jesus' "Reflection is carried on in the context of an evocation of the myth of the eschatological war." For Perrin,

> the use of Kingdom of Heaven (God) evokes the myth of the eschatological war between God and the powers of evil and interprets the fate of John the Baptist, and the potential fate of Jesus and his disciples as a manifestation of that conflict.[43]

In his interpretation of the Lord's Prayer in Luke 11:2-4, Perrin focused on the petition, "Thy kingdom come." In *Kingdom of God* he emphasized the tension in the prayer between the present and future as this is related to the experience of the individual. The same interpretation was offered in *Rediscovering*.[44] In *Language* Perrin interpreted "Thy Kingdom come" as evoking various expectations. He saw the other petitions of the prayer as expressions of these various expectations.

> Once it is recognized that Kingdom of God is being used as a tensive symbol in the opening petition of the prayer, then the remaining petitions become particularly interesting; they represent realistic possibilities for the personal or communal experience of God as king. God is to be experienced as king in the provision of "daily bread," in the experienced reality of the forgiveness of sins, and in support in the face of "temptation."[45]

After discussing the use of Kingdom of God in Jesus' teaching, Perrin proceeded to investigate how this symbol was used in subsequent Christian literature. He began with earliest Christianity, giving Luke 17:22-23 as an example. Here the earliest Christians use the symbol Son of man to evoke the myth of apocalyptic redemption where Jesus had used the symbol Kingdom of God to evoke the myth of the activity of God.

> The first major interpretation of Jesus' use of Kingdom of God in the Christian traditon is the interpretation of the coming of the Kingdom of God in terms of the coming of Jesus as Son of Man. This remains within the general framework of the myth of God as active on behalf of his people, but the change is unmistakable. The tensive symbolism has given way to the steno-symbolism more usual in Jewish and Christian apocalyptic.[46]

With Augustine the myth of God acting came to produce the speculative idea of the church as the Kingdom of God. Augustine called this the "city of God." The use of Kingdom of God as a reflective or speculative theological concept served Augustine by allowing him to give it a meaning consistent with his broader theological understanding. Augustine's approach, however, did not do justice to the literary features of the

---

[43]Ibid., 46.

[44]See Perrin, *Kingdom of God*, 191-93; *Rediscovering*, 160-61.

[45]Perrin, *Language*, 47.

[46]Ibid., 60.

Kingdom of God as symbol. In Perrin's opinion, "The direct reference to the symbol, and the evocation of the myth by the symbol is lost." Rather than evoking "the myth of the activity of God on behalf of his people" Augustine had chosen to reflect on the symbol and to speculate "about the relationship between the church and the kingdom."[47] The Kingdom of God continued to be seen as a speculative theological concept even to the modern period, as for example in Ritschl's notion that the Kingdom of God was the goal of God's redemptive activity and of the Christian community.

With the rise of the historical-critical method, it became possible to attempt to reach Jesus' use of the symbol. Johannes Weiss was one of the first to contribute to this attempt with his book, *Jesus' Proclamation of the Kingdom of God*. He understood the Kingdom of God as an apocalyptic conception on the lips of Jesus. Furthermore, he viewed Jesus' concept as irrelevant to his day and his theology. Perrin praised Weiss for providing a corrective to Ritschl, but found fault in his viewing the Kingdom of God as a concept.

> Kingdom of God is a symbol, and which functions by evoking a myth; a valid hermeneutical procedure must take these considerations very seriously into account. In practice everything turns upon the status of the myth; if the myth is held to be acceptable or meaningful then we have one hermeneutical possibility; if it is not so held then we have a second and very different one.[48]

Perrin discussed Walter Rauschenbusch as an example of the first hermeneutical possibility and Rudolf Bultmann as the pioneer of the second.

In his social gospel program Rauschenbusch accepted the ancient myth of God active in the world on behalf of the people. He spoke of "the energy of God realizing itself in human life"[49] and saw God at work in the social struggle of people. Perrin saw this direct use of the symbol as an appropriate option for those who were able to see the ancient myth it evoked as still meaningful for modernity.[50]

Bultmann felt that the ancient myth was no longer valid and so set forth an option different from that of Rauschenbusch, especially in *Jesus and the Word* and *Jesus Christ and Mythology*. Unlike Weiss, Bultmann sought to interpret this dead myth so that it could again have meaning. He arrived at what he felt to be Jesus' conception of life that was expressed in the myth. He described human life in modern nonmythical language in or-

---

[47]Ibid., 60-65; the quotation is taken from 64.

[48]Ibid., 69-70.

[49]Walter Rauschenbusch, *A Theology for the Social Gospel* (Nashville: Abingdon, 1919) 141; all of Perrin's quotations were taken from *A Gospel for the Social Awakening: Selections*.

[50]Perrin, *Language*, 70-71.

der to dispense with the mythical trappings. At the level of literary criticism Perrin criticized Bultmann's work because Bultmann saw Kingdom of God as a conception or, to use the terminology Perrin was using, as a steno-symbol. Likewise, he challenged Bultmann's understanding of myth, which he called an "allegorical myth." "In the case of a myth in which the symbols are steno-symbols," Perrin wrote, Bultmann's

> hermeneutical method would be appropriate, and if Jesus were proclaiming the coming of the Son of Man as the early church proclaimed that coming—i.e., with the "coming" functioning as a steno-symbol to be exhausted by one event on a calendar date in chronological time—then Bultmann would be correct. The non-occurrence of the expected event would discredit the myth and demand and expression of its implicit understanding of existence in non-mythological language. But it is my claim that Kingdom of God is not a steno-symbol in the message of Jesus, and that the myth involved is not allegorical myth.[51]

Perrin's approach did not require accepting the ancient myth and using the symbol as directly as Rauschenbusch but, unlike that of Bultmann, it did view the symbol as tensive and the myth as a way to understand human existence in the world. Perrin admitted that his view could lead to a result similar to Bultmann's understanding of the eschatology of Jesus. However, Perrin felt that he, unlike Bultmann, arrived at his result through an understanding of the Kingdom of God that took into account its relationship to symbol and myth.[52] "If 'Kingdom of God' is a 'steno-symbol' or 'sign' in the historical proclamation of Jesus," Perrin observed,

> then our hermeneutical responsibility is earnestly to look for signs of the end and busily to calculate dates for the coming of the Son of Man. But if it is a "tensive" or "true" symbol, then our responsibility is to explore the manifold ways in which the experience of God can become an existential reality to man.[53]

Perrin's interpretation of the Kingdom of God changed considerably with his utilization of literary criticism as a method. He first turned his attention to the Kingdom of God in *Kingdom of God*. There his concern was clearly on (1) reaching a knowledge of the historical Jesus' proclamation and, (2) interpreting that proclamation in such a way that it could be a continuing relevant ethic. He, of course, never explicity made the second point, but it is a valid one to make about his work. These same two concerns were at work in his second book, *Rediscovering*.

---

[51]See Perrin, *Language*, 71-80; the quotation is from 78.

[52]Ibid., 198-99.

[53]Norman Perrin, "Eschatology and Hermeneutics: Reflections on Method in the Interpretation of the New Testament," *Journal of Biblical Literature* 93 (March 1974): 13.

With *Language* Perrin shifted from a primary interest in the historical expression of the concept Kingdom of God in Jesus' proclamation to a primary interest in the continuing impact and relevance of the symbol. This shift was due to his adoption of literary criticism, his increasingly ahistorical theological perspective, and the difficulty of, on the one hand, accepting the apocalyptic nature of Jesus' proclamation while, on the other hand, attempting to relate it to a relevant ongoing ethic.

Perrin did not develop the final step in his hermeneutical program (which he called "hermeneutics") as it related to the Kingdom of God, other than to say we must "explore the manifold ways in which the experience of God can become an existential reality to man."[54] Presumably, this is the responsibility of each person who is encountered by the symbol, Kingdom of God, and the myth it evokes of God's activity. His position did clear the way for making this exploration into the many ways God can be known.

In addition to being a noticeable development in his own work on the Kingdom of God, *Language* represented a significant contribution in the scholarly discussion. Of the biblical literary critics Perrin was the first to suggest how general literary-critical principles could be useful in interpreting the Kingdom of God. His book is certainly not the last word on a literary-critical view of the Kingdom of God. It is, however, a good first step in opening up the Kingdom of God to literary-critical perspectives.

---

[54]Ibid.

A CHARACTERISTIC FORM
OF THE TEACHING:
THE PARABLES

• The Continental Discussion. •

Adolf Jülicher's pivotal two-volume work on the parables in 1888 and 1889[1] marked the beginning of modern parable interpretation.[2] His study was the decisive revision of the allegorical interpretation that had held sway since the early church fathers. Jülicher's primary concern and his most important contribution was his argument that each of the parables of Jesus was indeed a parable with an easily recognized point rather than an allegory with many mysterious points. In providing a history of the interpretation of Jesus' parables, he was able to show that by taking them as allegories the church had offered numerous confusing and contradictory interpretations. Jesus' parables, though, were not designed to confuse the hearer. They were simple and vivid stories taken from the everyday life of the time to make a single point about the Kingdom of God. Jülicher's discussion of the Good Samaritan (Lk 10:29-37) is a good example of his treatment of the parables.[3] He called it a vivid story that could have happened. Its point, he added, is that it is an example of the ideal

---

[1]Adolf Jülicher; *Die Gleichnisreden Jesu*, 2 vols. (Tübingen: J. C. B. Mohr, 1888, 1889). Jülicher published an earlier book on the parables in 1886, but the two-volume work is considered his most important statement.

[2]For example, Warren S. Kissinger, *The Parables of Jesus: A History of Interpretation and Bibliography*, ATLA Bibliography Series 4 (Metuchen NJ: Scarecrow Press and American Theological Library Association, 1979) xiii.

[3]Where possible, the parable of the Good Samaritan will be used to illustrate the interpretative approach of each.

neighbor as one who is loving and compassionate and not necessarily one who is born in the upper class.[4]

The form-critical study of the parables was the next major advance in understanding their historical context and expression. Among the early form critics, Bultmann made the most important contribution. In *History of the Synoptic Tradition*[5] he traced the development of the parabolic traditions by identifying those elements he considered to be secondary. For him, secondary elements could include a parable's setting, allegorical expansion, and other minor features.

Two other form critics, C. H. Dodd and Joachim Jeremias, both of whom wrote books on the parables, made important strides in uncovering their history. Benefiting from the contributions of Jülicher, Bultmann, and others, Dodd in *The Parables of the Kingdom* stressed that the parables must be interpreted in their historical context in the life of Jesus. Dodd saw this setting to be the great eschatological act of God, interpreted in terms of his notion of "realized eschatology." His insight had the effect of moving interpretation away from a moralistic tone.[6]

Because of his theological position that the historical Jesus is crucial for faith, Jeremias in *The Parables of Jesus* continued Dodd's attempt to set the parables firmly in the context of the life and teaching of Jesus. He agreed with Dodd that eschatology was the key to understanding Jesus' parables, but he modified Dodd's perspective by taking seriously the futuristic emphasis. He also emphasized that, for the most part, the parables are apologetic in that they reflect conflict in Jesus' ministry as he spoke in vindication of the gospel. Hearers felt compelled to respond to Jesus' proclamation about the Kingdom of God. Jeremias peeled off the various layers of material added to the parables by the early church, finding a number of ways in which that church transformed them.[7]

All of these scholars were interested to some degree in the continuing relevance of the parables. In more recent parable interpretation, however, this concern for continuing relevance has been pursued with much more intensity and has found expression in new hermeneutical approaches. The first important effort to exhibit a concern for the continuing relevance of the parables was the "new hermeneutic," a movement

---

[4]See *Die Gleichnisreden Jesu* 2:585-98 for Jülicher's treatment of the Good Samaritan.

[5]See Rudolf Bultmann, "Similitudes and Similar Forms," in *The History of the Synoptic Tradition*, rev. ed., trans. John Marsh (New York: Harper and Row, 1963 [1921]) 166ff, esp. 179ff. on form and history.

[6]C. H. Dodd, *The Parables of the Kingdom*, rev. ed. (New York: Charles Scribner's Sons, 1961 [1935]) 13.

[7]Joachim Jeremias, *The Parables of Jesus*, 6th ed., trans. S. H. Hooke. (New York: Charles Scribner's Sons, 1963 [1947]).

that began in the mid-1950s with Ernst Fuchs.[8] Fuchs set out to (1) determine Jesus' understanding of his own existence and (2) analyze the parables as "language events" (*Sprachereignisse*). The best way to accomplish the first objective, he wrote, was by working on the second. He viewed Jesus' parables as comparisons or analogies. As analogies, parables have a "picture-half" and a "reality-half" and the reality-half comes to expression at the point of comparison (*tertium comparationis*). The parables, then, indicate to us Jesus' understanding as well as provide us with the opportunity to share that understanding.

Eta Linnemann in *Jesus of the Parables* continued the discussion along the same lines as Fuchs. Like Jeremias, Dodd, and others, she stressed the importance of acknowledging the historical context of the parable as first told by Jesus. She also stressed that the original language event can be repeated through preaching. When this repetition occurs, the parable as a language event creates new possibilities for the hearer. Most of *Jesus of the Parables* was devoted to an interpretation or what she called an exposition of the parables. In her exposition of the Good Samaritan, she retold the parable, paying particular attention to the historical referents of the story and the "event" nature of the original telling. Through this exposition, she saw the parable as challenging persons toward acting as the Samaritan did—toward authentic living. This and other challenges of Jesus' parables are extremely radical in nature and cannot be reduced to simple moral admonitions.[9]

Eberhard Jüngel was the third new hermeneutic scholar who had an interest in parables. In his major book, *Paulus und Jesus,* he reiterated many of the themes common to persons writing in the new hermeneutic tradition. With regard to the parables, the one point at which he forged ahead of his new hermeneutic colleagues was in viewing the parables as bringing the Kingdom of God to language (*zur Sprache*). This affirmation was an important development because he affirmed that he denied the validity of the distinction Fuchs made between the "reality-half" and the "picture-half" of the parable. Jüngel viewed this distinction as an unfortunate legacy stemming from Jülicher. Jüngel's insight was an important development which foreshadowed the literary critics who later said that the distinction between form and content was the greatest hindrance to understanding the parables.[10]

In summary, the new hermeneutic's major contribution to the study of Jesus' parables was in its attention to language. Bultmann drew on the

---

[8]Fuchs's major work is *Hermeneutik,* 2nd ed. (Bad Cannstatt: R. Müllerschön Verlag, 1958 [1954]). Many of his essays have appeared in *Studies of the Historical Jesus.*

[9]Eta Linnemann, *Jesus of the Parables: Introduction and Exposition,* 3rd ed. (New York: Harper & Row, 1966 [1961]).

[10]Eberhard Jüngel, *Paulus und Jesus* (Tübingen: J. C. B. Mohr, 1967 [1962]).

existentialist categories of the earlier writings of Martin Heidegger, but the new hermeneutic—itself a development of Bultmann's work—drew on Heidegger's later work, in which he examined language as a manifestation of Being. Appreciation for the significance of language and its form in interpreting the parables found particular expression in the work of the literary critics.

Norman Perrin's first major discussion of the parables came in *Rediscovering the Teaching of Jesus*. He used two parables, one from the Mekilta on Exodus 20:2 and one from Jesus (Mt 11:16-19), to illustrate his interpretation of the parables. The parable from the Mekilta reads:

> I am the Lord thy God
>   Why are the Ten Commandments not said at the beginning of the Torah? They give a parable. To what may this be compared? To the following: A king who entered a province said to the people: "May I be your king?" But the people said to him: "Have you done anything good for us that you should rule over us?" What did he do then? He built the city wall for them, he brought in the water supply for them, and he fought their battles. Then when he said to them: "May I be your king?" They said to him, "Yes, yes," Likewise, God. He brought the Israelites out of Egypt, divided the sea for them, sent down the manna for them, brought up the well for them, brought the quails for them, he fought for them the battle with Amalek. Then he said to them: "I am to be your king." And they said to him: "Yes, yes."[11]

Perrin suggested that one should find the analogous situation between the parable and the audience in order to understand the point of the comparison, which is the message of the parable. In the example from the Mekilta, the analogous situations are the king and the people, and God and the Israelites. Since this is a parable and not an allegory, the king is not God and the people of the province are not the Israelites.[12]

The example from Matthew 11:16-19 (Children in the Marketplace) is an exception to the rule of Jesus' parables because it is the only clear synoptic parable where the parable and the analogous situation to which it originally referred are given in the same context.

> But to what shall I compare this generation? It is like children sitting in the market place and calling to their playmates, "We piped to you, and you did not dance; we wailed; and you did not mourn." For John came neither eating nor drinking, and they say, "He has a demon"; the Son of man came eating and drinking, and they say, "Behold, a glutton and a drunkard, a friend of tax collectors and sinners!" Yet wisdom is justified by her deeds.

---

[11]As reproduced in Norman Perrin, *Rediscovering the Teaching of Jesus* (New York: Harper and Row, 1976 [1967]) 84.

[12]Ibid.

Perrin went on to suggest that Jesus may have deliberately ended his parables so as to allow his hearers to grasp the point and to find the parallel or analogy for themselves. "The primary task of the exegete of the parables," he wrote, "is to set the parable in its original context in the ministry of Jesus so that, by an effort of historical imagination, he may grasp the crucial point of the parable itself and then find the parallel or analogy to which it is directed."[13] Perrin aimed to determine the main point of each parable and then to group the parables in categories based on their messages. Two groups of parables are concerned with the proclamation of the Kingdom of God. They emphasize the joyousness with which the activity of God may be experienced, as in the Hidden Treasure (Mt 13:44; Thomas 98:30-99:2) and Pearl (Mt 13:45; Thomas 94:14-18) and parables that express the challenge of the forgiveness of sins, such as the Lost Sheep (Lk 15:1-7), Lost Coin (Lk 15:8-10), and Prodigal Son (Lk 15:11-32).[14]

The remaining four groups of parables were placed under the category of recognition and response to the Kingdom proclamation. For example, the Children in the Marketplace is concerned to warn against preconceived ideas that blind one to the reality of the Kingdom challenge. Here Perrin drew on Jeremias's work to show that this story refers to certain children who find fault with other children who do not participate in play activities. Some found fault with John because he was an ascetic and found fault with Jesus because he was not. In this way the parable warns of preconceived ideas about Jesus.[15]

The Good Samaritan was one of the parables told to depict the necessary response to the Kingdom challenge, and Perrin's treatment of it illustrates his interest in the historical form, context, and message of the parables. He joined Linnemann in understanding the question "who is my neighbor?" as an editorial addition by Luke. He also suggested, with Bultmann, that the admonition "go and do likewise" was probably added by the church during the parable's transmission. Concentrating on the parable as told by Jesus, he attempted to determine its life situation. Like Manson and Jeremias, he stressed the vivid or realistic details of the parable and viewed this characteristic as evidence for authenticity.

Perrin proceeded to determine what the parable must have meant when it was first told. He pointed out that the original hearers would have expected an Israelite layman to be the third character because the Jews and Samaritans hated one another. The parable must have been a great "shock" to the hearers in Jesus' day. Perrin did not elaborate on the "shocking" nature of the parable, but this suggestion can be seen as an-

---

[13]Ibid., 87.

[14]Ibid., 83.

[15]Ibid., 85-86; 119-21.

ticipating his literary-critical approach to the parables in *Jesus and the Language of the Kingdom*. According to him, the parable teaches "that the crucial aspect of human relationships is response to the neighbor's need."[16] His conclusion at this point is not all that different from Jülicher's conclusion that the parable teaches that the ideal neighbor is loving and compassionate. Finally, Perrin made the point that the teaching of the parable must be set in the context of Jesus' Kingdom proclamation of the forgiveness of sins and his table fellowship with tax collectors and sinners.

• The American Reformulation •

The most important recent attempt to interpret the parables in a manner that attributes to them continuing relevance has been that of the American biblical literary critics. This hermeneutical approach to the Bible drew its important interpretive principles from the American New Criticism. Like the critics of other literature, the biblical literary critics were reacting against what they saw as an overemphasis on historical criticism. The principal interpreters of the parables all had training in the historical-critical method. They did not deny that method, but they did say that it failed to go far enough. In addition to their general tendency to minimize history, a tendency shared with the critics of other literature, the biblical critics were also confronted with the apocalyptic teaching of the parables. Although they did not say so, their emphasis on the parable as a continuing work of art rather than as a source for Jesus' apocalyptic proclamation conveniently avoided the embarrassment of a mistaken Jesus. In addition to their dependence on the New Criticism, the biblical critics, as I will demonstrate, drew on new hermeneutic insights in general, and the new hermeneutic existentialist perspective in particular. Four of the most important biblical literary critics were Amos N. Wilder, Robert W. Funk, Dan O. Via, Jr., and John D. Crossan.

Amos Wilder's *Early Christian Rhetoric* first appeared in 1964, the first major contribution to a thoroughgoing literary approach to the parables. As a poet and literary critic Wilder was sensitive to the power of language and metaphor and he brought to the parables this sensitivity, which thus far had been absent. Although he discussed the parables only briefly, his comments were influential in the subsequent development of parable interpretation.

Wilder's most important contribution was his insistence that no clear distinction could be made between form and content. He spoke of the "revelatory character" of Jesus' parables and urged the use of "metaphor" in speaking of the parables. As "extended metaphors," the parables actually participate in and enable the hearers to participate in the reality to which they refer.

---

[16]Ibid., 124.

> Now we know that a true metaphor or symbol is more than a sign, it is a bearer of the reality to which it refers. The hearer not only learns about that reality, he participates in it. He is invaded by it. Here lies the power and fatefulness of art. Jesus' speech had the character not of instruction and ideas but of compelling imagination, of spell, of mythical shock and transformation.[17]

Wilder also stressed the realism of the parables, as had Dodd, Jeremias, and others. They are "human and realistic" and their "secularity" helps us to recognize Jesus the "layman."[18] The parables challenge every person to make a judgment and come to a decision. Although Wilder's emphasis was on the parable as a literary object which mediates reality, one should realize that his ultimate concerns were historical and expositional. He wanted to reach the creative vision of Jesus the author of the parables and then enable the modern hearer to share that vision of reality.

If Wilder suggested the direction in which literary criticism of the parables should go, it was Robert W. Funk who began to move in that direction by showing how it could be done. He devoted Part II of his three-part *Language, Hermeneutic, and Word of God* to the parables of Jesus, making several important points about the parable as metaphor. The parable is a metaphor extended to realistic narrative. This realistic narrative draws the reader into it as participant and produces an identification with the characters and situation of the parable. The parable has unlimited potential for new meaning because that meaning is dependent on the way the metaphor is viewed in the new historical situations of the readers.

Although the parable can have hundreds of possible meanings because of the possible new situations, there is an original meaning that can be determined by historical criticism. Funk stated that this original meaning should act as a control over the reinterpretation of the parable. The focus of his interpretation, though, was clearly on allowing the parable as metaphor to speak in a new way in a new circumstance. He made the point that a simile illustrates meaning but that a metaphor creates the potential for new meaning by showing a familiar world and then challenging the reader's imagination by turning that world upside down.

> The parables as pieces of everydayness have an unexpected "turn" in them which looks through the commonplace to a new view of reality. This "turn" may be overt in the form of a surprising development in the narrative, an extravagant exaggeration, a paradox; or it may lurk below the surface in the so-called transference of judgment for which the parable calls. In either

---

[17]Amos N. Wilder, *Early Christian Rhetoric: The Language of the Gospel*, rev. ed. (Cambridge MA: Harvard University Press, 1971 [1964]) 84.

[18]Ibid., 73, 74.

case the listener is led through the parable into a strange world where everything is familiar yet radically different.[19]

In his "reading" of the Good Samaritan[20] Funk attempted to recreate the effect the story had on the original hearers. The reader is invited to participate in the parable by identifying with the man in the ditch and by being shocked at the supposed inappropriate responses to his plight by the priest, Levite, and Samaritan. The commonplace nature of the parable is shattered by juxtaposing the Samaritan's response with that of the priest and Levite. By identifying with the man in the ditch, the reader experiences the parable and new meaning is created.

In addition to his own work on the parables, Funk was instrumental in inaugurating a Society of Biblical Literature seminar on the parables. The work of the seminar, which included Funk, Perrin, Wilder, John D. Crossan, Dan O. Via, Jr., James M. Robinson, and Jack Dean Kingsbury, was published in *Semeia,* a special journal series sponsored by the Society of Biblical Literature.

In *The Parables,*[21] Via continued the intensive literary-critical analysis of the parables found in Funk's book. Published one year after Funk's, this book included an extended consideration of what Via called a "literary-existential analysis" of parables. He provided a careful criticism of the "severely historical approach" to the parables that he said had failed to do justice to their aesthetic nature, thereby ignoring their relevance to persons outside the parables' historical context. He insisted that his literary approach overcame the limitations of historical criticism by viewing the parable as existing in its own right, autonomous and independent of its author. He showed how this could be done by providing a detailed literary analysis of the parable as a self-contained aesthetic object in which various elements are integrated into a connected whole.

The "existential" aspect of Via's approach surfaced in his attempt to show that the parable has an understanding of existence that each reader could relate to his own understanding of existence. Via utilized the new hermeneutic term "language event" to suggest that the parables introduce a new way of understanding one's situation. In addition, the parables as language events invite the hearers to make a decision concerning the new possibility confronting them in the parable.

Via's literary-existential analysis involved an understanding of the movement of the plot and the character activity of the parable. He iden-

---

[19]Robert W. Funk, *Language, Hermeneutics and the Word of God: The Problem of Language in the New Testament and Contemporary Theology* (New York: Harper and Row, 1966) 161.

[20]Ibid., 199-222; see also "Good Samaritan as Metaphor," Funk's contribution to *Semeia* 2 (1974).

[21]Dan O. Via, Jr., *The Parables: Their Literary and Existential Dimension* (Philadelphia: Fortress Press, 1967).

tified two kinds of plot movement in the parable—the comic and the tragic. The ontological possibility of gaining existence was expressed in the comic parables where the protagonist moves upward toward well-being and integration into a positive society as in the Workers in the Vineyard (Mt 20:1-16), Unjust Steward (Lk 16:1-9), and Prodigal Son (Lk 15:11-32). The possibility of losing existence was expressed in the tragic parables where the protagonist falls toward catastrophe and isolation from society, as in the Talents (Mt 25:14-30; Lk 19:12-27), Ten Maidens (Mt 25:2-12), Wedding Garment (Mt 22:11-14), Wicked Tenants (Mt 21:33-46; Mk 12:1-11; Lk 20:9-19; Thomas 93:1-18), and Unforgiving Servant (Mt 18:23-25).

Only in the last chapter of *Parables* did Via discuss the historical Jesus, a discussion not necessary for the argument of his book. The location of this chapter and its unnecessary relationship to the other chapters is an indication of the direction literary criticism of the parables was taking. Literary concerns were overshadowing historical concerns.

In addition to his book on the parables, Via was a member of the Society of Biblical Literature's Parables Seminar and contributed an article to *Semeia* I.[22] By this time he had developed a structuralist approach to the parables and his article is a "literary-structural approach" (as opposed to his earlier "literary-existential analysis") to the Good Samaritan. First, he distinguished between the discourse with the scribe (Luke 10:25b-37) and the story or parable proper (10:30-35). He brought to the story a structuralist grid, presupposing that all stories are variations on the fundamental patterns he was using.

Finally, Crossan's major contribution can be found in *In Parables*, where he emphasized that a parable is a metaphor. Drawing on his critical knowledge of poetry, Crossan further refined Jülicher's distinction between parable and allegory. In contrast to allegory, a parable, like a symbol, expresses what cannot be expressed any other way, requires a right "instinct" for understanding (not right "knowledge"), partakes of the reality it renders intelligible, and invites participation in its referent. Like a myth, in contrast to allegory, a parable reveals something not reducible to clear language. Furthermore, the parable as metaphor functions so that "participation precedes information."[23] The metaphor creates a new possibility and invites the reader to participate in its referent. The subtitle of Crossan's book, *The Challenge of the Historical Jesus*, indicates his interest in Jesus as author of the parables. It is possible and legitimate to view the parables as expressions of Jesus' experience of God. In this emphasis Crossan differed from Via, who stressed that the parables are nonreferential.

---

[22]Dan O. Via, Jr., "Parable and Example Story: A Literary-Structuralist Approach," *Semeia* 1 (1974): 222-35.

[23]John Dominic Crossan, *In Parables: The Challenge of the Historical Jesus* (New York: Harper and Row, 1973) 14.

Crossan identified three parables, the Hid Treasure (Mt 13:44; Thomas 98:30-99:2), Pearl of Great Price (Mt 13:45; Thomas 94:14-18), and Great Fish (Thomas 81:28-82:3), as "key" parables that are paradigmatic of our experience of the Kingdom and of the other parables. These three parables contain a structural sequence—advent of a new world and unforeseen possibilties, reversal of the entire past, and action or the expression of the new world and the new possibilities—that can be used to categorize other parables of Jesus.

Crossan's exegesis of the Good Samaritan provides a good example of how he interpreted each parable according to its category. In the Good Samaritan the reader is forced to say what cannot be said: good plus Samaritan. Crossan related enough of the historical referents of the parable to show why good plus Samaritan was a dramatic reversal of the original hearer's world view. The "good" (priest and Levite) becomes bad and the "bad" (Samaritan) becomes good. In struggling with this reversal, the reader would be experiencing the in-breaking of the Kingdom of God. He continued his historical study of the Good Samaritans by pointing out how the parable was changed to an example story as Christianity moved further into a Gentile environment where terms like "Samaritan" were not fully understood.

Perrin's discussion of the parables in the last stage of his scholarly pilgrimage was set firmly in the context of his association with the biblical literary critics. That discussion came in *Jesus and the Language of the Kingdom*, a book that reflected a decided shift in approach from his earlier works in *Rediscovering*. Perrin's discussion of parables in *Language* was more a survey of modern parable research with an emphasis on American literary-critical analysis than it was a statement of his own position. Yet, his critical survey of the scholarly discussion clearly indicated the direction in which his own thought was moving.

Perrin utilized his four-step "hermeneutical process" to evaluate various modern interpreters of the parables. He paid some attention to the first two steps of the process—textual and historical criticism. However, his main interest was clearly on evaluating modern research with respect to the last two steps—literary criticism and hermeneutics.[24] Perrin credited Jülicher, Dodd, and especially Jeremias with making great strides in the textual and historical criticism of the parables. His criticism of their work was at the level of literary analysis. For example, Jeremias's passion for the historical setting hindered him from fully appreciating the parables as literary entities with an ongoing life of their own. Perrin said the new hermeneutic, while making certain gains, especially in its concern for dialogue between text and interpreter (what Perrin called "herme-

---

[24]Norman Perrin, *Jesus and the Language of the Kingdom: Symbol and Metaphor in New Testament Interpretation* (Philadelphia: Fortress Press, 1976) 89-90.

neutics"), also failed to grasp the essence of the parable as a literary entity.[25]

In Perrin's judgment, the weakest link in parable interpretation had been literary criticism and the related issue of hermeneutics. It was the American biblical literary critics, especially Wilder, Funk, Via, and Crossan, who were, according to Perrin, overcoming the deficiency in parable interpretation.

Although Wilder provided very little exegesis of the parables, Perrin considered his hermeneutical reflections to be extremely important and influential on the subsequent discussion because "he taught us to see the significance of the literary factors."[26] This was important for Perrin because it led to a view of the parables in which they were seen to have an ongoing life and vitality of their own.

Perrin credited Funk with moving the discussion ahead by showing how the parables have an ongoing life and vitality. Funk's emphasis on the parable as metaphor and on the reader as participant corresponds to Perrin's categories of literary criticism and hermeneutics. Perrin was particularly impressed with Funk's intepretation of the Good Samaritan.

Perrin considered Via's *Parables* to be the most important book about the parables since the work of Jeremias. Via had moved the discussion forward in terms of seeing the parable as a metaphor *extended to narrative*. But Perrin saw the "existentialist" aspect of Via's literary-existentialist analysis as a failure at the level of hermeneutics. "There is a sense in which after we have learned all that we can about a text with the aid of our critical tools we have to allow that text to address us once more as a text," Perrin wrote. But, he added,

> Via does not do this. Having learned what he can about the text by the aid of his critical tools, he then discards that text and concerns himself with things that can be learned from it. In the last resort this does not seem to be a hermeneutical procedure adequate to the parables.[27]

Again, as with the new hermeneutic, Perrin argued that one must cultivate a literary or artistic sensibility rather than a rational one, to fully appreciate the parables.

Crossan was, according to Perrin, the second (Via the first) of the "two leading American interpreters of the parables."[28] Unlike Via, Crossan made a contribution at the level of a historical understanding of the parables. Crossan's concentration on the Treasure, Pearl, and Great Fish as "key" parables and his emphasis on advent-reversal-action as the way to

---

[25]Ibid., 91ff., 107ff.

[26]Ibid., 131.

[27]Ibid., 155.

[28]Ibid., 155-156.

view the parables and the message of Jesus were important contributions, according to Perrin, at the level of historical criticism. But at the level of hermeneutics Perrin gave Crossan poor marks. Crossan's "concern is for the meaning of the text on the lips of Jesus." Perrin wrote. "His whole endeavor is to make possible a sophisticated understanding of the parable as Jesus taught it." Yet, Perrin added, Crossan never "self-consciously addresses the problem of the final act of interpretation of the text into the present of a contemporary reader."[29]

These remarks about Crossan's work at the level of hermeneutics do not seem to be justified. Crossan's emphasis on the parable as metaphor invited the reader to participate in its referent. His exegesis of the Good Samaritan suggested that the reader could experience the Kingdom of God by virtue of his participation in the parable. But Perrin's criticism of Crossan shows him to be concerned with both literary criticism and hermeneutics in the interpretation of the parables.

Perrin's treatment of the parables is important because it provides another example of the way his interpretation of a significant issue shifted in the context of his methodological and theological pilgrimage. In *Rediscovering* he stated that the primary task of the exegete of the parables "is to set the parable in its original context in the ministry of Jesus so that . . . he may grasp the crucial point of the parable."[30] Here he was reflecting the same general concern as the Continental scholars who emphasized historical setting. By the time he wrote *Language* he had shifted toward an ahistorical theological perspective. The parables (along with the Kingdom of God), because of their natural literary qualities, provided an excellent opportunity to make use of the literary-critical method.

---

[29]Ibid., 168.

[30]Perrin, *Rediscovering*, 87.

PART III

PERRIN
AND
AMERICAN
BIBLICAL
HERMENEUTICS

TOWARD AMERICAN
BIBLICAL HERMENEUTICS

In surveying biblical interpretation today in light of Perrin's intellectual pilgrimage, several important and related issues merit exploration, all of which have significance for American biblical hermeneutics. First, all interpreters must address the theological implications of ahistorical approaches to studying the biblical text. Perrin's movement from history to text enables us to see clearly the difficulties of locating meaning in history. While he seemed to be approaching a synthesis that would have reincorporated history and theology, his emphasis at the end of his career was clearly on the text as a literary entity. This is especially evident in *Jesus and the Language of the Kingdom,* where Perrin understood the Kingdom of God and the parables as essentially autonomous literary objects.

For the later Perrin, for structuralists, and other literary critics who take ahistorical stances, the theological question becomes: Is it possible to be Christian without reference to the Jesus of history, indeed, without reference to a biblical text understood in the framework of history? The question is not a new one. It had been raised in response to Bultmann's program of demythologizing. Fritz Buri, Schubert Ogden, and Karl Jaspers had argued that consistency dictated that Bultmann's approach led to the dissolution of any uniqueness to faith as Christian. The new questers had raised the same issue, although their agenda, of course, was to save Christ from becoming just another mythological notion.

While the question is not new, it does take a novel form today. Bultmann saw the gospels as myths; contemporary literary critics see them as literary objects. There is an important distinction, however. Bultmann's concern was to interpret the myths existentially and in this case, at least according to the left-wing Bultmannians, Christ is dissolved and the important point becomes the existential encounter. In the literary approach Christ remains because form and content are inseparable. We can compare literary criticism at this point with the program of Hans W. Frei who, from a different angle, but one with affinities to the New Criticism, has argued that it is unnecessary to demythologize the gospel stories. Using their imaginations, readers can participate in the "realistic narratives" of the gospels.[1]

Admittedly, the distinction between Christ showing up in a myth that is translated into an existential encounter and Christ showing up in a text that is appreciated purely for its form is rather fine. The finer the distinction one would see here, the less it is possible to view strictly literary approaches to the Bible as fostering encounters with the text that are necessarily Christian. I do see a distinction, however slight, and therefore affirm that strictly literary approaches can remain Christian precisely because the form of the text is respected and retained. On the other hand, the shift from a historical to a literary paradigm as a possible occasion for faith is certainly a significant one with important implications.

This shift brings in a definite element of universalism. A historical event by definition is limited to particular space and time and, appropriately, a religion based on what its adherents understand to be special historical occurrences tends toward exclusivism. When the referent of the text is intrinsic—that is, the form of the text itself—rather than extrinsic—that is, a Christ-event of history—there is no space-time limitation placed on its occurrence. The form of Christ can occur in various times and various places and, indeed, has done so since the first forms (the gospels) came into existence. Texts (or paintings or music for that matter) interpreted as purely aesthetic objects are free from the space and time constraints of history.

In the introduction to this "Studies in American Biblical Hermeneutics" series,[2] Charles Mabee calls for biblical hermeneutics that will release the Bible into a public reading. In his own contribution to this series, Mabee regards science and technology as foundational and fundamental drives in American society and he uses them as an entry point into the development of American biblical hermeneutics.[3] He pursues this technological/scientific mentality by conceiving America as a scientific "experiment" that seeks to find the universal nature of humanity. He seeks to relate the metaphor of universal scientific and technological experiment, which is America, to the Judeo-Christian tradition with its inherent particularism. Taking a literary-critical approach to the Bible is one way to join the universal and the particular, to use Mabee's categories. As

---

[1]See especially Hans W. Frei, *The Eclipse of Biblical Narrative* (New Haven: Yale University Press, 1974); and *The Identity of Jesus* (Philadelphia: Fortress Press, 1975).

[2]Charles Mabee, *Reimagining America: A Theological Critique of the American Mythos and Biblical Hermeneutics* (Macon GA: Mercer University Press, 1985) xi.

[3]Ibid., xiii-xv; and Mabee's subsequent unpublished paper, "The Bible: From the Church to the World," read at the 1985 Society of Biblical Literature/American Academy of Religion Southeastern Region meeting.

suggested above, a text, conceived as a literary object, retains its original form and hence at one level its particularity, and, at the same time, is loosed from the space-time constraints of history and into a more public and universal setting.

In addition to and related to their universal orientation, science and technology are primary elements in what has been widely recognized as an increasingly secular climate in this country, a definite movement from "sacred to profane," to borrow a phrase from the late William A. Clebsch.[4]

To science and technology I would add pluralism as an important factor in the secular trend. Peter Berger interprets secularization as a loss of transcendence and views pluralization as supporting the secular trend because it erodes the cohesive communities that provide "a stable social-psychological base . . .for meta-empirical certitudes."[5] While science, technology, and pluralism are certainly prominent themes in European culture, America is a microcosm of what has occurred in Western culture at large.

The evolution of religion in America, the "sacred" side of the sacred-profane continuum, has paralleled this secular turn. The exploding plethora of denominations and sects, the fundamentalist-modernist controversies, and the separation of church and state concept are but three of the many manifestations of the puralism, scientific mentality, and secularism that is the American story. Religion itself, as both a reflection of and meaningful partner in the secularization process, has had to change and grow with the times. When it resists, it is reduced to cultlike status and consigned to the fringes of American life. Hence David Tracy's suggestion in *The Analogical Imagination*, appropriately subtitled *Christian Theology and the Culture of Pluralism*, that theology must speak to three different publics: society, academy, and church.[6] Tracy's model can appropriately be applied to American biblical hermeneutics. In an increasingly secular culture the Bible, if it is to remain a classic text and gain the public hearing Charles Mabee calls for, must be interpreted in a fashion that releases it into the "profane" realm. If not, the Bible will become the church's

---

[4]See William A. Clebsch, *From Sacred to Profane in America* (New York: Harper and Row, 1968).

[5]Peter L. Berger, "For a World with Windows: Hartford in Sociocultural Context," *Against the World, For the World: The Hartford Appeal and the Future of American Religion*, ed. Peter L. Berger and Richard J. Neuhaus (New York: Seabury, 1976) 11.

[6]David Tracy, *The Analogical Imagination: Christian Theology and the Culture of Pluralism* (New York: Crossroads Press, 1981) 1-46. Unlike Harvey Cox, in *Religion in the Secular City: Toward a Postmodern Theology* (New York: Simon and Schuster, 1984), I see the current revival of conservative/fundamentalist religion as a relatively short-lived aberration of the secular trend in the modern and postmodern world.

book in such a way and to such a degree that it becomes privatized and isolated, thereby losing its classic status.

Canonical criticism, typified in Brevard S. Childs' *Introduction to the Old Testament as Scripture* and his more recent *The New Testament as Canon*[7] can be criticized along these lines. While canonical criticism does offer the possibility of releasing the text into the *believing* community in a fresh new way, the eventual cost may very well be to intensify the sacred/secular dichotomy and further remove the Bible from the general public, especially if its proponents neglect serious dialogue with the larger community of critics.[8]

Perrin's lifework can serve as a catalyst for the development of a hermeneutic that both speaks to and is an appropriate and helpful reflection of secularization in general and the scientific/technological/pluralistic spirit in particular. While his untimely death kept him from constructing anything like a complete theory of interpretation, the direction and thrust of of his pilgrimage in hermeneutics, and especially his concern with literary criticism toward the end of his life, provide a clue to a hermeneutic that can effectively release the Bible into a public reading in American society. History and theology, when conceived together, result, I suggest, in religious exclusivism. Literary criticism, which severs the text from history and theology, relates much better to a secular and pluralistic context.

Perrin's literary-critical turn begins to do for hermeneutics what the death-of-God theologians were trying to do for theology in the 1960s. The death-of-God theology was an inevitable fruit of the steady eclipse of the supernatural in the Western world since the Enlightenment. The radical theologians severed Christianity from its historical and metaphysical roots in order to construct a truly secular theology. In light of our concern with literary criticism and American biblical hermeneutics, it is interesting that the death-of-God theology was largely American-based and that language and literature played a primary role. Thomas J. J. Altizer's fascination with Blake, his turn to language and, more recently, deconstruction,[9] and Paul van Buren's long interest in linguistic analysis[10] are but two examples of this phenomenon.

---

[7]Brevard S. Childs, *The New Testament as Canon: An Introduction* (Philadelphia: Fortress Press, 1985).

[8]John Priest, "Canon and Criticism: A Review Article," *Journal of the American Academy of Religion* 48 (June 1980): 259-71, suggests that as canonical criticism develops, its advocates may forget the hardwon gains of historical-critical scholarship.

[9]For Altizer's interest in language see *The Self-Embodiment of God* (New York: Harper & Row, 1977), *Total Presence: The Language of Jesus and the Language of Today*

While literary approaches to the Bible may potentially release the "sacred" text to the "secular" society, I can make no claim that such an approach arises purely out of the "sacred" end of the spectrum. In fact, the New Criticism itself, despite what some of its advocates contend, is in a sense a reflection of the secular technological spirit; likewise, psychological behavorism, built as it is on the notions of stimulus-response and the more extreme examples of computer art and music. As part of his sustained attack on much twentieth-century criticism, Gerald Graff records the critique of New Criticism by Susan Sontag, Richard Poirier, and others and points out that "all of them agree that New-Critical style objective interpretation is an extension of the Western technological mentality with its aggressive need to transform its world into objects."[11] These critics decry such an "extension" of Western aggressiveness, but that aggressive mentality is not necessarily to be viewed negatively. It can be seen simply as the culture speaking to itself—interpreting itself—and in this instance using a classic text, the Bible, to do so.

It is, however, at this very point, where literary criticism is conceived as technique only, that its reading of texts exhibits a decided weakness. A text, so read, is prohibited a forward look to possible spheres of meaning for those who encounter the text. This is certainly unacceptable for interpreting the Bible for the public of the church because of the Bible's role as sacred text; but it is also unacceptable for interpreting the Bible for the public of society as a whole because of the Bible's role as a classic text in Western literature.

Perrin recognized this limitation of a strict literary approach and in his four-step hermeneutical process—textual criticism, historical criticism, literary criticism, and hermeneutics—was beginning to rectify it. Here he was explicitly concerned with the question of how the fruits of exegesis are to be appropriated. He called this "hermeneutics proper," the final step in his four-step process, and defined it as the "dynamic interaction between text and interpreter," contending that the three previous steps were subordinate to the final step and designed to serve it. He never lived to develop his understanding of hermeneutics proper or of its specific relationship of the literary-critical step in interpretation. However he was, at his death, directing a dissertation of the parables that provides evidence of his concern of combine literary criticism with hermeneutics

---

(New York: Seabury, 1980), and "History as Apocalypse," in *Deconstruction and Theology* (New York: Crossroad, 1982) 147-77.

[10]See Paul M. van Buren, *The Secular Meaning of the Gospel: Based on An Analysis of Its Language* (New York: Macmillan, 1963); and *The Edges of Language: An Essay in the Logic of a Religion* (New York: Macmillan, 1972).

[11]Gerald Graff, *Literature Against itself: Literary Ideas in Modern Society* (Chicago: University of Chicago Press, 1979). 130.

proper. Mary Ann Tolbert begins her study of the parables with a "primary question."

> What can the parables mean today? To investigate this question, the parables themselves will be considered as literary texts with a certain timeless dimension rather than as historical artifacts of a long dead culture, and the general field of literary criticism will supply our major methodological and ideological foundations.[12]

In the hermeneutical discussions that have continued unabated since Perrin's death, the issue of how literary criticism can be conceived within a larger hermeneutical theory has been central. In her perceptive analysis of literary criticism, Lynn Poland has recently and cogently argued the weakness of a literary criticism narrowly conceived as formalism. By formalism or formalist literary criticism she means those literary theories that focus on the intrinsic or internal structure of a work. Like Gerald Graff and Murray Krieger[13] she finds an inconsistency in the writings of the formalist critics who say, on the one hand, that poetry gives knowledge about being human but, then, on the other hand, advocate a theory of autonomy and a critical process that prohibits such knowledge from being revealed. Poland shows the New Criticism severs the text from extrinsic spheres of meaning and, therefore, neglects whatever value the text might have for the experience of being human in the world.

> The central difficulty . . . is that the centripetal focus of New Critical theory—its stress on the autonomy, self-sufficiency, and objectivity of the literary work of art—tends to prevent literature from exercising those cognitive and thus transformative powers which this theory also wishes to claim for it.[14]

Poland suggests that this deficiency in formalist theory can be corrected by combining it with Bultmann's hermeneutical model, which, standing alone, is inadequate because it fails to probe the revelatory and transformative potential of language.

> Bultmann's hermeneutical program and formalist theory stand, in a sense, in inverse relation: each provides a dimension which the other inadequately develops. In its capacity to explicate how poetic language can disclose the "new" in a way that other discourse cannot, formalism can assist

---

[12]Mary Ann Tolbert, *Perspectives on the Parables: An Approach to Multiple Interpretations* (Philadelphia: Fortress Press, 1979) 13-14. Compare Dan O. Via's *The Parables: Their Literary and Existential Dimension* (Philadelphia: Fortress Press, 1967).

[13]Graff, *Literature Against Itself*, 37, 133ff.; Krieger, *The New Apologists for Poetry* (Minneapolis: University of Minnesota Press, 1956).

[14]Lynn Poland, *Literary Criticism and Biblical Hermeneutics: A Critique of Formalist Approaches*, American Academy of Religion Academy Series 48 (Chico CA: Scholars Press, 1985) 159.

in constructing a theory of the language of faith. Insofar as formalism ignores the problems of interpretation, Bultmann's reflections on hermeneutical issues are formalism's complement.[15]

To lay the groundwork for a biblical hermeneutic that can fruitfully join formalist theory with Bultmannian existentialist interpretation, Poland turns to the interpretation theory of Paul Ricoeur. With respect to the questions at hand, Ricoeur's specific and primary interest is struturalism, on the one hand, and the existential and ontological traditions stemming from Heidegger and Gadamer, on the other. By viewing structuralism as an extreme form of New Critical formalism, Poland can utilize Ricoeur's program in her reflections on biblical hermeneutics. The key, for Poland, is Ricoeur's notion that the object of understanding is the world which is projected through the structure of a work. In this Ricoeurean extension of the New Criticism, then, the interpreter participates in the structure of a text, moving eventually to the world it projects—a world which, according to Poland, "finally forms and transforms the self of the reader according to its intention."[16]

Perrin's discussion of the final step in his hermeneutical process made clear his indebtedness to Bultmann's existentialism. While Perrin is to be commended for beginning to press the issue of how the fruits of exegesis are to be appropriated, I question his uncritical acceptance of existentialism as the conceptual scheme by which to understand the hermeneutical moment. Bultmann naturally adopted an existentialist interpretation because that philosophy informed the mood of his day. While it is certainly not time for it to be discarded, the limitations of existentialism's exaggerated individualism require it to make room for the full range of interpretative possibilities. The mood of our time, for example, is more socially conscious. Liberation theologians, including blacks, feminists, and representatives of the third world, are raising questions about the nature of human beings and about the religious traditions that will probably not be completely satisfied by an existentialist interpretation. Once we break the hold of existentialist interpretation, which Perrin never did, we pave the way for the hermeneutical moment to take a social, psychological, mystical, political, or ecclesiastical form or a combination of these or other perspectives. The appropriation is truly informed by the listening of the reader and his or her particular situation and not by a forced preunderstanding.

Poland's use of Bultmann's existentialist approach, unlike that of Perrin, is critical and shows the beginnings of a carefully worked out hermeneutic. However, it is clear that Bultmann's legacy lives on and one might ask whether it is possible to remain so fully committed to the ex-

---

[15]Ibid., 67.

[16]Ibid., 189.

istentialist paradigm and still make the necessary room for other perspectives.

At some point in discussions of hermeneutical theory it is helpful to turn to specific texts to illustrate a particular approach. Perrin's primary focus in his literary-critical phase was on the Kingdom of God and parables. In his discussion of the Kingdom of God, Perrin's newfound literary sensibilities, combined with his keen historical eye, led him to the conclusion that the Kingdom of God was a tensive symbol on the lips of Jesus. He did not, however, leave his investigation there. In *Jesus and the Language of the Kingdom* he pursued the way this symbol has been viewed in selected interpreters from subsequent generations, with a view toward its continuing significance. His brief but perceptive comments on Augustine, Weiss, Ritschl, Rauschenbusch, and Bultmann set the stage for his challenge to explore the manifold ways the symbol can have significance.

James Goss provides an example of how a literary reading can be utilized in an interpretation that extends the appropriation of a text beyond existentialism's narrow confines. He joins a literary reading of Kingdom of God, and especially Perrin's view of the Kingdom as a tensive symbol, to an interpretation that combines existentialism (following Bultmann) and Carl G. Jung's theory of individuation. Specifically Goss contends that the metaphorical quality, or tensiveness, of the Kingdom does justice to the "otherness" of the Kingdom while recognizing its power to initiate a response within the self in terms of individuation.[17]

The question now posed to American biblical hermeneutics is how this symbol, understood tensively, can be utilized fruitfully in a reading that presupposes the American context. H. Richard Niebuhr's *The Kingdom of God in America*[18] comes immediately to mind as a successful attempt to interpret the various meanings of Kingdom of God in American Christianity—as "sovereignty of God," as "reign of Christ," as "Kingdom on earth." What is needed in American biblical hermeneutics is to turn from thinking about Kingdom of God in American Christianity to Kingdom of God in America.

Some help may be found in the category "American Civil Religion." Civil religion has been an often debated notion since the term was first thrust into the scholarly limelight in 1968 by Robert Bellah.[19] Discussion

---

[17]James Goss, "Eschatology, Autonomy, and Individuation: The Evocative Power of the Kingdom," *Journal of the American Academy of Religion* 49 (September 1981) 363-81.

[18]Richard Niebuhr, *The Kingdom of God in America* (New York: Harper and Brothers, 1937).

[19]See Robert N. Bellah, "Civil Religion in America," in *Religion in America*. ed, William G. McLoughlin and Robert N. Bellah (Boston: Houghton Mifflin, 1968) 3-23.

has turned on such questions as whether civil religion was being described or being advocated, the value of the category for interpreting the American story, and the exact nature of civil religion. American civil religion, if it is conceived as a constructive and interpretative category, can be fruitfully utilized to appropriate the tensive symbol Kingdom of God to America. Literary criticism in effect would be providing a biblical hermeneutical base for constructive civil religion.

When the Kingdom of God is seen as tensive and as an autonomous literary object, however, the biblical text or biblical symbol may be naively reduced to "whatever you want it to mean"—only now via a more sophisticated understanding of literature. When such a notion, along with the power that religious symbols can carry, is applied to any particular societal context, with its attendant political, racial, and economic agendas, the danger is evident and shows up in the form of temptation to offer a religious justification for certain attitudes and actions. Our present and past are full of examples of such unwelcome excesses.

If there is a central weakness in Poland's reflections on hermeneutics, it is at this very point. She correctly works to extend literary criticism to look forward in order to open the way for meaning and significance. But does she, in so doing, adequately safeguard such a hermeneutic from resulting in such a subjective interpretation of a text that the text itself becomes at best irrelevant and at worst a justification for some selfish end? In the last paragraph of her book Poland points out that Ricoeur's program takes little account of the place of historical, form, and redaction criticism in the interpretative process. She does not, however, suggest how such a weakness can be overcome.

Again Perrin provides a clue toward correction of this deficiency. Even though he had become fascinated with literary-critical questions, there are good indications that at the very end of his life Perrin was planning to reincorporate the historical-critical concerns that had consumed so much of his lifework. When a concern for the history and theology of the text is given adequate weight, it minimizes the danger that the text will end up meaning just what one wants it to mean. In his four-step hermeneutical process, Perrin gave attention to historical criticism, under which he placed form and redaction analysis, and, just as important, his own scholarship over the years testifies to the fact that he was willing and able to do more than pay lip service to these stages of interpretation. His four-step process is designed as a rough guide to lead the interpreter through the steps necessary to fully encounter a text in all its facets.

Ricoeur's interpretative theory provides an opportunity to conceive more philosophically how authorial meaning can somehow be related to contemporary understanding. Poland is correct to point out that Ricoeur pays very little attention to the original meaning of a text. In his dialectic of explanation and understanding, his primary concern is with structural analysis and existential/ontological understanding. He plainly says the author's intention is "beyond our reach" and this is one factor that makes "guessing the meaning of a text" necessary.[20] Yet, Ricoeur at times leaves a crack in the door leading to original meaning. The transition from speaking to writing "alters" and "transforms" the message, but this "does not imply that the notion of authorial meaning has lost all significance," he says.[21] With the New Critics Ricoeur is certainly wary of the intentional fallacy; but he is also cognizant of what he calls

> the fallacy of the absolute text: the fallacy of hypostasizing the text as an authorless entity. If the intentional fallacy overlooks the semantic autonomy of the text, the opposite fallacy forgets that a text remains a discourse told by somebody, said by someone to someone else about something. It is impossible to cancel out this main characteristic of discourse without reducing texts to natural objects, i. e., to things which are not man-made, but which, like pebbles, are found in the sand.[22]

Again I make no attempt to suggest that a text's original meaning has played a significant role in Ricoeur's hermeneutics. It has not. But his view that the "world of the text" occupies the space between the author and contemporary reader paves the way for a true "fusion of horizons" (Gadamer's *Horizonverschmelzung*) between the writer and the reader whereby information uncovered by the historical critic can be legitimately taken into account in one's intepretation of a text. Perrin's four-step process can be viewed as a more specific theoretical formulation of Ricoeur's emphasis on the world of the text, a formulation that allows a creative tension between original meaning and contemporary relevance.

Ricoeur and the New Critics are correct to be suspicious about our ability to uncover the original meaning of an ancient text. However, ex-

---

[20]Paul Ricoeur, *Interpretation Theory: Discourse and the Surplus of Meaning* (Fort Worth: Texas Christian University Pess, 1976) 75.

[21]Ibid., 29-30. Cf. Ricoeur's recent brief article "From Proclamation to Narrative," *The Journal of Religion* 64 (October 1984): 501-512, where, utilizing process terminology, he probes how historical "occasions," uncovered or rediscovered by Perrin and Jeremias, relate to narrative in the gospel tradition. The recent work of Perrin's student, Werner H. Kelber, in *The Oral and the Written Gospel: The Hermeneutics of Speaking and Writing in the Synoptic Tradition, Mark, Paul, and Q* (Philadelphia: Fortress Press, 1983), supports Ricoeur's view that the move from speaking to writing radically alters the message. Kelber draws on contemporary oral theory, as exampled in the work of W. J. Ong, to call into question the "disproportionately print-oriented hermeneutic" of most biblical study (xv). His investigation into the orality of the gospel tradition, by the way, leads him to suggest that the Jesus of history was of no import to the tellers and hearers of the gospel stories and, therefore, that the modern attempt to identify "authentic" sayings is misconceived (71).

[22]Ibid., 30. For a good summary of Ricoeur's work as it relates to biblical interpretation, see Lewis S. Mudge, in Paul Ricoeur, *Essays on Biblical Interpretation*, Lewis S. Mudge, ed. (Philadelphia: Fortress Press, 1980) 1-40. See also *"Paul Ricoeur on Biblical Hermeneutics,"* in *Semeia* 4 (1975).

treme skepticism in this regard is unwarranted. As Perrin pointed out, historical-critical methods are highly developed and open to use by anyone willing and able to do so. "There is nothing esoteric or private about historical criticism," Perrin wrote; "its conclusions are openly arrived at by methods common to historical scholarship as such, so that a consensus as to the historical understanding of a given text should be possible among competent historical scholars."[23] To use Ricoeur's terms, we never reach verification; but our validation of an interpretation that takes account of history becomes more sure.

To illustrate how a concern for original meaning can contribute to interpretation that also pays attention to the text as literature, I turn to the Kingdom of God. According to Perrin, on the lips of Jesus the tensiveness of this symbol worked against any particular identification of God's activity with the nationalistic hopes of the Jews, who in the apocalyptic traditions looked for a dramatic irruption of God into history. In appropriating (or understanding, to use Ricoeur's term) the Kingdom of God, the interpreter is, on the one hand, free to explore the manifold ways the symbol can have significant while, on the other hand, being restrained from making an appropriation which is selfishly conceived and absolutely fixed. In the context of American biblical hermeneutics there is at least the possibility that the symbol can serve as an interpretative tool without being used to justify narrow agendas.

While Perrin is to be commended for moving beyond an undue emphasis on history and theology, the direction and thrust of his pilgrimage, and especially his later reconsideration of the role of history, serves to caution us about an excessive reliance on language. A strictly literary paradigm, while providing a valuable corrective to the dominance of history, will ultimately prove unable alone to bear the full hermeneutical burden. Two reasons make this true. First, such a paradigm, whether it comes in the guise of New Criticism or structuralism, prohibits a forward look to possible spheres of meaning for those who encouner the text as well as a backward look to the historical event that precipitated it.

Second, interpretative approaches that rely primarily on a literary paradigm—or any other single paradigm for that matter—fail to recognize fully a fundamental characteristic of the Bible that has been known since the rise of modern criticism; that is, that the Bible consists of widely diverse genres of literature. While some texts are amenable to New Critical inquiry, others are not. The varied biblical corpus has yet to be exhausted by a single interpretative approach. By glancing only at the history of the exegetical methods Perrin was most familiar with one can see that certain methods have generally been associated with particular texts or particular groupings of texts. For example, form criticism focused on iso-

---

[23]Norman Perrin, *Jesus and the Language of the Kingdom: Symbol and Metaphor In New Testament Interpretation* (Philadelphia: Fortress Press, 1976) 4.

lated gospel pericopes while redaction criticism stepped back to see the gospels as wholes and then, from this new perspective, saw the individual pericopes in new ways. New Testament literary criticism has naturally gravitated to the Kingdom of God symbol and to parables as literary entities. Structural, reader-response, rhetorical, canonical, and other forms of criticism, likewise, develop favorite texts or groupings of texts and each, standing alone, tends to develop its own canon within a canon.

In formulating his four-step hermeneutical process Perrin was, in large part, responding to what he saw as a methodological crisis in biblical studies; in this regard his voice is not alone. Viewing the current scene as a crisis, however, is an interpretation that can be called into question. The "crisis" exists only in our interpretation—in our language. This particular interpretation results in part from a preoccupation with method itself, perhaps stemming from our "scientific" mentality with its passion for total explanation.

When we begin to recognize that the diverse nature of the biblical materials is in part responsible for the variety of approaches, the interpretation of the current scene as one of crisis begins to lose its hold and new possibilities for understanding open up. An alternative to the crisis mentality is to take the view that the current scene is very healthy. We do not need some new metamethod that will replace outdated approaches (though methodological advances are always welcome) nor do we need a "new Bultmann" to forge a new era in appropriating the text to modernity.

At the present moment the most pressing task in biblical studies is to consolidate the enormous gains made in the modern period and to interpret those gains in such a way as to foster additional advances. Since the methods afield today require a high degree of technical expertise—and no single exegete can master them all—one way to consolidate our gains is to increase the level of conversation among biblical scholars working from various perspectives. Historical scholarship must be conceived as to make full room for literary approaches. Likewise, literary criticism in whatever form must be tempered by appropriate grounding in historical research.

Although Perrin was motivated in part by a desire to break through what he saw as a methodological impasse by forging yet another approach, his four-step hermeneutical process does provide a clue to a kind of model that can foster needed dialogue among those working from various stances. Such conversation is especially necessary when a particular text or genre of a text lends itself to multiple angles of interpretation—as do the parables, which have fruitfully yielded to form, redaction, literary, and structural criticism.

Attempts to apply the fruits of exegesis creatively to various interpretative possibilities are welcome and are consistent with the hermeneutical impulse I see stemming from Perrin's synthesis. The probability that a text's meaning is maximized is enhanced when that meaning emerges out of a text read from a potentially multifaceted exegetical base. The probability that the appropriation of that meaning is maximized is enhanced when it is refined through interaction with various preunderstandings. Biblical studies in America, with its current pluralism of approaches, is an excellent place to experiment with and forge out a truly ecumenical hermeneutic.

I am suggesting an attitudinal stance toward hermeneutics rather than a well-defined model of interpretation. Every encounter between text and reader becomes an occasion for the hermeneutical moment to occur in new and perhaps surprising ways. Interpretation becomes dynamic and open-ended, and its quality is dependent on a configuration of things that includes the interpretive possibilities the reader brings to the text as well as the revelatory potential of the text itself. When flexibility and openness rather than rigidity and closure, dialogue rather than monologue, characterize our reading of the text, we approach a hermeneutic that, rather than a clearly defined formula, truly becomes a process.

Perrin's pilgrimage has proven to be paradigmatic of the direction and thrust of biblical studies in the twentieth century. His pilgrimage, and especially his attempt to construct a hermeneutic that does justice to various interpretative approaches, which for him included the historical, theological, and literary, is also prophetic. It is prophetic in the sense of foreshadowing a new age when biblical hermeneutics advances beyond a reductionism that relies on single approaches and toward a multifaceted and enriched hermeneutic that results from and contributes to true dialogue among interpreters and the texts before them.

•BIBLIOGRAPHY•

• I. Works by Perrin •

A. Books, Articles, and Book Reviews
(Listed in chronological order.)

"The Kerygmatic Theology and the Question of the Historical Jesus." *Religion in Life* 29 (Winter 1959-1960): 86-97. Coauthored with William R. Farmer.

Review of *Die Heidenmission in der Zukunftschau Jesu*, by David Bosch. *Journal of Biblical Literature* 79 (June 1960): 188-89.

"New Testament Studies Today." *Candler Advocate* 3 (1961): 2-3; 10-11.

Review of *Exegetische Versuche und Besinnungen*, I, by Ernst Käsemann. *Journal of Biblical Literature* 80 (September 1961): 294-95.

"Faith, Fact and History." *Christian Advocate* 6 (20 December 1962): 7-8.

Understanding the Teaching of Jesus. New York: Seabury Press, 1983. Edited by David Abernathy, based on a 1962 lecture series by Norman Perrin entitled "The Teaching of Jesus."

Review of *Die Auslegung der Versuchungsgeschichte unter besonderer Berücksichtigung der Alten Kirche*, by Klaus-Peter Köppen; and *La Tentation de Jésus dans l'interprétation patristique de Saint Justin à Origène*, by M. Steiner. *Journal of Biblical Literature* 81 (December 1962): 426-27.

Review of *Human Achievement and Divine Vocation in the Message of Paul*, by William A. Beardslee. *Emory University Quarterly* 18 (1962): 60-61.

The Kingdom of God in the Teaching of Jesus. New Testament Library. London: SCM Press; Philadelphia: Westminster Press, 1963.

Review of *New Frontiers in Theology* 1: *The Later Heidegger and Theology*, ed. James M. Robinson and John B. Cobb. *Christian Advocate* (7 November 1963): 19-20.

Review of *Historical Tradition in the Fourth Gospel*, by C. H. Dodd. *Journal of Religion* 44 (October 1964): 335.

"The Challenge of New Testament Theology Today." *Criterion* 4 (Spring 1965): 25-34. Reprinted in *New Testament Issues*, ed. Richard Batey, 15-34. New York: Harper & Row, 1970.

"Against the Current," A review of *Jesus and the Kingdom*, by George E. Ladd. *Interpretation* 19 (April 1965): 228-31.

Review of *Bible Key Words from Kittel* 5. *Christian Advocate* (30 December 1965): 18.

Review of *Jesus and Christian Origins*, by Hugh Anderson. *Journal of Religion* 45 (July 1965): 254-55.

"A Pertinent Distinction." Review of *The So-Called Historical Jesus and the Historic Biblical Christ*, ed. and trans. Carl E. Braaten. *Christian Century* 82 (17 February 1965): 214.

Review of *Esegetische Versuche und Besinnungen* 2, by Ernst Käsemann. *Journal of Biblical Literature* 84 (March 1965): 62-63.

Review of *The Relevance of Apocalpytic*, 3rd ed., rev., by H. H. Rowley: and *The Method and Message of Jewish Apocalyptic*, by D. S. Russell. *Journal of Religion* 45 (April 1965): 165-66.

Review of *The Setting of the Sermon on the Mount*, by W. D. Davies. *Journal of Religion* 45 (April 1965): 54.

"Mark 14:62: The End Product of a Christian Pesher Tradition." *New Testament Studies* 12 (1965-1966): 150-55. Also in *A Modern Pilgrimage in New Testament Christology*, 10-22. Philadelphia: Fortress Press, 1974.

"The Son of Man in Ancient Judaism and Primitive Christianity: A Suggestion." *Biblical Research* 11 (1966): 17-28. Also in *A Modern Pilgrimage in New Testament Christology*, 23-40. Philadelphia: Fortress Press, 1974.

"The Quest Simplified." Review of *Finding the Historical Jesus*," by J. F. Peter. *Christian Century* 83 (2 March 1966): 273-74.

"The *Wredestrasse* Becomes the *Hauptstrasse*: Reflections on the Reprinting of the Dodd *Festschrift*." *Journal of Religion* 46 (April 1966): 296-300.

"Wrestling with History," A review of *The Bible in Modern Scholarship: Papers Read at the 100th Anniversary of the Society of Biblical Literature*. ed. Philip Hyatt. *Christian Century* 83 (6 April 1966): 433.

Review of *Heilsgeschehen und Geschichte: Gesammelte Aufsätze, 1933-1964*, by Werner G. Kümmel. *Journal of Religion* 46 (April 1966): 335.

Review of *The Temptation and Passion*, Society for New Testament Studies Monograph Series 2, by Ernest Best. *Journal of Religion* 46 (April 1966): 318-19.

Review of *Easter Faith and History*, by Daniel P. Fuller; *The Question through the Centuries*, by Harvey K. McArthur; and *Finding the Historical Jesus*, by J. F. Peter. *Journal of Religion* 46 (July 1966): 396-99.

"Lukan New Wave," A review of *Studies in Luke-Acts*, ed. Leander Keck and J. Louis Martyn. *Christian Century* 83 (7 September 1966): 1081-82.

"New Beginnings in Christology," A review of *The Foundations of New Testament Christology*, by R. H. Fuller. *Journal of Religion* 46 (October 1966): 491-96.

Review of *Introduction to the New Testament*, by Paul Feine, Johannes Behm, and Werner G. Kümmel. *Journal of Religion* 46 (October 1966): 506-507.

Rediscovering the Teaching of Jesus. New Testament Library. London: SCM Press; New York: Harper and Row, 1967. Paperback ed., with new preface; New York: Harper and Row, 1976. *Was lehrte Jesus wirklich? Rekonstruktion und Deutung*, trans. P. Nohl. Göttingen: Vandenhoeck und Ruprecht, 1972.

Review of *Invitation to the New Testament*, by W. D. Davies. *Journal of Religion* 47 (January 1967): 82.

"The Parables of Jesus as Parables, as Metaphors, and as Aesthetic Objects: A Review Article." *Journal of Religion* 47 (October 1967): 340-46.

"Biblical Scholarship in a New Vein," A review of *The Parables: Their Literary and Existential Dimension*, by Dan O. Via, Jr. *Interpretation* 21 (October 1967): 465-69.

"Recent Trends in Research in the Christology of the New Testament." In *Transitions in Biblical Scholarship*, ed. J. Coert Rylaarsdam, 217-33. Essays in Divinity 6. Chicago: University of Chicago Press, 1968. Also in *A Modern Pilgrimage in New Testament Christology*, 41-56. Philadelphia: Fortress Press, 1974.

"The Son of Man in the Synoptic Tradition." *Biblical Research* 13 (1968): 1-23. Also in *A Modern Pilgrimage in New Testament Christology*, 57-83. Philadelphia: Fortress Press, 1974.

"The Creative Use of the Son of Man Tradition by Mark." *Union Seminary Quarterly Review* 23 (1967-1968): 357-65. Also in *A Modern Pilgrimage in New Testament Christology*, 84-93. Philadelphia: Fortress Press, 1974.

"Theological Impasse," A review of *Memory and Hope*, by Dietrich Ritschl. *Christian Century* 85 (10 April 1968): 456-57.

"Putting Back the Clock," A review of *Jesus—God and Man*, by Wolfhart Pannenberg. *Christian Century* 85 (11 December 1968): 1575-76.

"The Composition of Mark 9:1." *Novum Testamentum* (1969): 67-70.

The Promise of Bultmann: The Promise of Theology, ed. Martin E. Marty. Philadelphia: J. B. Lippincott, 1969; reprint, Philadelphia: Fortress Press, 1979.

What is Redaction Criticism? Guides to Biblical Scholarship, ed. Dan O. Via, Jr. Philadelphia: Fortress Press, 1969.

Review of *The Son of Man in Mark*, by Morna D. Hooker. *Journal of the American Academy of Religion* 37 (March 1969): 92-94.

Review of *Salvation in History*, by Oscar Cullmann. *Journal of Religion* 49 (July 1969): 303-305.

Review of *The Prayers of Jesus*, by Joachim Jeremias. *Journal of Religion* 49 (October 1969): 406-407.

"The Literary *Gattung* 'Gospel'—Some Observations." *Expository Times* 82 (1970): 4-7.

"The Use of [para]didonai in Connection with the Passion of Jesus in the New Testament." In *Der Ruf Jesu und die Antwort der Gemende für Joachim Jeremias,* ed. Eduard Lohse, Christoph Burchard, and Berndt Schaller, 204-12. Göttingen: Vandenhoeck und Ruprecht, 1970. Also in *A Modern Pilgrimage in New Testament Christology,* 94-103. Philadelphia: Fortress Press, 1974.

Review of *The Synoptic Gospels*, by Claude G. Montefiore; and *Studies in Pharisaism and the Gospels,* by I. Abrahams. *Journal of Religion* 50 (January 1970): 118-19,

Review of *Jesus in the Church's Gospels: Modern Scholarship and the Earliest Sources,* by John Reumann. *Encounter* 31 (Winter 1970): 73.

"The Christology of Mark: A Study in Methodology." *Journal of Religion* 51 (July 1971): 173-87. Translated as "Die Christologie des Markusevangeliums: Eine methodologische Studie." In *Das Markus-Evangelium*, ed. R. Pesche, 356-76. Darmstadt: Wissenschaftliche Buchgesellschaft, 1979. Also in *A Modern Pilgrimage in New Testament Christology,* 104-21. Philadelphia: Fortress Press, 1974. Also in *The Interpretation of Mark, Issues in Religion and Theology 7,* ed. William Telford, 95-108. Philadelphia: Fortress Press; London: SPCK, 1985.

"Towards an Interpretation of the Gospel of Mark." In *Christology and a Modern Pilgrimage: A Discussion with Norman Perrin,* ed. Hans Dieter Betz, 1-78. Claremont CA: Scholar's Press, 1971.

Review of *The Kingdom of God in the Synoptic Tradition,* by Richard Hiers. *Interpretation* 25 (1971): 223.

Review of *The Good News According to Mark,* by Eduard Schweizer, trans. by D. H. Madvig. *Journal of Religion* 51 (October 1971): 310-11.

Review of *Synoptische Quellenanalyse und die Frage nach dem historischen Jesus,* by Martin Lehmann. *Journal of Biblical Literature* 90 (1971): 374.

Review of *The Christology of Early Jewish Christianity,* by Richard N. Longenecker. *Church Quarterly* 3 (1971): 246-47.

"The Modern Interpretation of the Parables of Jesus and the Problem of Hermeneutics." *Interpretation* 25 (April 1971): 131-48.

Review of *Early Christian Experience,* by Günther Bornkamm. *Journal of Religion* 51 (July 1971): 222.

"Reflections on the Publication in English of Bousset's *Kyrios Christos.*" *Expository Times* 82 (August 1971): 340-42.

Review of *Sacramentum Verbi: An Encyclopedia of Biblical Theology,* ed. J. B. Bauer. *Christian Century* 88 (20 October 1971): 1237-38.

"Wisdom and Apocalyptic in the Message of Jesus." In *The Society of Biblical Literature One Hundred and Eighth Annual Meeting: Proceedings 2*, 543-72. Society of Biblical Literature, 1972.

"The Evangelist as Author: Reflections on Method in the Study and Interpretation of the Synoptic Gospels and Acts." *Biblical Research* 17 (1972): 5-18.

"Unraveling the Tangled Skein." Review of *Trajectories through Early Christianity*, by James M. Robinson and Helmut Koester. *Interpretation* 26 (April 1972): 212-15.

"Historical Criticism, Literary Criticism, and Hermeneutics: The Interpretation of the Parables of Jesus and the Gospel of Mark Today." *Journal of Religion* 52 (October 1972): 361-75.

Review of *The New Testament Christological Hymns*, by Jack T. Sanders. *Journal of Religion* 52 (October 1972): 459-61.

"Bultmann, Rudolf." In *Encyclopedia Britannica: Macropaedia* 3:478-79. 15th ed. (1974).

"Eschatology and Hermeneutics: Reflections on Method in the Interpretation of the New Testament." *Journal of Biblical Literature* 93 (March 1974): 3-14.

"The Contours of a Pilgrimage," In *A Modern Pilgrimage in New Testament Christology*, 1-9. Philadelphia: Fortress Press, 1974.

"Reflections from a Way Station." In *A Modern Pilgrimage in New Testament Christology*, 122-32. Philadelphia: Fortress Press, 1974.

A Modern Pilgrimage in New Testament Christology. Philadelphia: Fortress Press, 1974.

The New Testament: An Introduction—Proclamation and Parenesis, Myth and History. New York: Harcourt Brace Jovanovich, 1974. Revised as Norman Perrin and Dennis Duling, *The New Testament: An Introduction—Proclamation and Parenesis, Myth and History*, 2nd ed. New York: Harcourt Brace Jovanovich, 1982.

"The Christology of Mark." In *L'Evangile selon Marc. Tradition et rédaction*, ed. M. Sabbe, 471-85. Leuven: Leuven University Press, 1974.

Review of *Studien zur Passionsgeschichte*, by Eta Linnemann. *Biblica* 55 (1974): 132-34.

"The Interpretation of a Biblical Symbol." *Journal of Religion* 55 (July 1975): 348-70.

"Jesus and the Theology of the New Testament." Paper presented at the 38th annual meeting of the Catholic Biblical Association, Denver, Colorado, 19 August 1975. Published in *Journal of Religion* 64 (October 1984): 413-31.

"Mark, Gospel of." In *The Interpreter's Dictionary of the Bible*, Supplement: 571-73. Nashville: Abingdon Press, 1976.

"Secret, Messianic." In *The Interpreter's Dictionary of the Bible,* Supplement: 798-99. Nashville: Abingdon Press, 1976.

"Son of Man." In *The Interpreter's Dictionary of the Bible,* Supplement: 833-36. Nashville: Abingdon Press, 1976.

"The Interpretation of the Gospel of Mark." *Interpretation* 30 (April 1976): 115-24.

"The High Priest's Question and Jesus' Answer (Mark 14:61-62)." In *The Passion in Mark,* 80-95, ed. Werner H. Kelber. Philadelphia: Fortress Press, 1976.

Jesus and the Language of the Kingdom: Symbol and Metaphor in New Testament Interpretation. Philadelphia: Fortress Press, 1976.

The Resurrection According to Matthew, Mark, and Luke. Philadelphia: Fortress Press, 1977. Published in the United Kingdom as *The Resurrection Narrative: A New Approach.* London: SCM Press, 1977.

B. Translations

"The Qumran Texts and the New Testament," by Joachim Jeremias. *Expository Times* 70 (December 1958): 68-69.

"The Lord's Prayer in Modern Research," by Joachim Jeremias. *Expository Times* 71 (February 1960): 141-46.

The Sermon on the Mount, by Joachim Jeremias. London: Athlone Press, 1961; Philadelphia: Fortress Press, 1963.

The Problem of the Historical Jesus, by Joachim Jeremias. Philadelphia: Fortress Press, 1964.

The Eucharistic Words of Jesus, 3rd ed., by Joachim Jeremias. London: SCM Press; New York: Charles Scribner's Sons, 1966.

• II. Works by Other Scholars •

Abernathy, David. *Understanding the Teaching of Jesus.* New York: Seabury Press, 1983. Based on a 1962 lecture series, "The Teaching of Jesus," by Norman Perrin.

Achtemeier, Paul. *Introduction to the New Hermeneutic.* Philadelphia: Westminster Press, 1969.

Beardslee, William A. *Literary Criticism of the New Testament.* Guides to Biblical Scholarship, ed. Dan O. Via, Jr. Philadelphia: Fortress Press, 1970.

Betz, Hans Dieter, ed. *Christology and a Modern Pilgrimage: A Discussion with Norman Perrin.* Claremont CA: Scholar's Press, 1971.

Boers, Hendrikus. *What is New Testament Theology? The Rise of Criticism and the Problem of a Theology of the New Testament.* Guides to Biblical Scholarship. Philadelphia: Fortress Press, 1979.

Bornkamm, Günther. *Jesus of Nazareth,* trans. Irene and Fraser McLuskey with James M. Robinson. New York: Harper and Row, 1960 [1956].

Bradbury, John M. *The Fugitives: A Critical Account*. Chapel Hill: University of North Carolna Press, 1958.

Brooks, Cleanth, Jr. *The Well Wrought Urn: Studies in the Structure of a Poem*. New York: Regnal and Hickcock, 1947.

_____, and Robert Penn Warren. *Understanding Fiction*. New York: F. S. Crofts, 1943.

_____. *Understanding Poetry*. New York: Henry Holt, 1938.

Bultmann, Rudolf. *Existence and Faith: Shorter Writings of Rudolf Bultmann*, trans. Schubert Ogden. Cleveland: World, 1960.

_____. *Faith and Understanding*, 6th ed., trans. Louise P. Smith. London: SCM Press, 1969 [1966].

_____. *The History of the Synoptic Tradition*, rev. ed., trans. John Marsh. New York: Harper and Row, 1963 [1921].

_____. *Jesus Christ and Mythology*. New York: Charles Scribner's Sons, 1958.

_____. *Jesus and the Word*, trans. Louise P. Smith and Erminie H. Lantero. New York: Charles Scribner's Sons, 1934 [1926].

_____. "New Testament and Mythology." In *Kerygma and Myth*, ed. Hans Werner Bartsch, trans. Reginald H. Fuller, 1-44. New York: Harper and Row, 1961 [1941].

_____. "The Primitive Christian Kerygma and the Historical Jesus," trans. Carl E. Braaten and R. A. Harrisville. In *The Historical Jesus and the Kerygmatic Christ: Essays on the New Quest of the Historical Jesus*, 15-42. Nashville: Abingdon Press, 1964.

_____. *Theology of the New Testament*, 2 vols., trans. Kendrick Grobel. New York: Charles Scribner's Sons, 1951, 1955.

Carlston, Charles E. "A Positive Criterion of Authenticity?" *Biblical Research* 7 (1962): 33-44.

Ciardi, John, and Miller Williams. *How Does a Poem Mean?* 2nd ed. Boston: Houghton Mifflin, 1975 [1959].

Cobb, John B., and James M. Robinson, eds. *The New Hermeneutic*. New York: Harper and Row, 1964.

Conzelmann, Hans. *Jesus*, trans. J. Raymond Lord. Philadelphia: Fortress Press, 1973 [1959].

_____. *An Outline of the Theology of the New Testament*, 2nd ed. Trans. John Bowden. New York: Harper and Row, 1969 [1968].

_____. *The Theology of St. Luke*, trans. Geoffrey Buswell. New York: Harper and Brothers., 1960 [1954].

Crossan, John D. *In Parables: The Challenge of the Historical Jesus*. New York: Harper and Row, 1973.

_____. "Literary Criticism and Biblical Hermeneutics." *Journal of Religion* 57 (January 1977): 76-80.

_____, ed. *Paul Ricoeur on Biblical Hermeneutics. Semeia* 4 (1975).

_____. *Raid on the Articulate: Comic Eschatology in Jesus and Borges.* New York: Harper and Row, 1976.

Dewey, Kim E. "Peter's Curse and Cursed Peter (Mark 14:53-54, 66-72)." In *The Passion in Mark: Studies on Mark 14-16,* ed. Werner H. Kelber, 96-114. Philadelphia: Fortress Press, 1976.

Dibelius, Martin. *From Tradition to Gospel,* rev. ed., trans. Bertram L. Woolf. New York: Charles Scribner's Sons, 1935 [1919].

_____. *Jesus,* trans. Charles B. Hendrick and Frederick C. Grant. Philadelphia: Westminster Press, 1949 [1939].

Dodd, C. H. *The Parables of the Kingdom,* rev. ed. New York: Charles Scribner's Sons, 1961 [1935].

Donahue, John R. *Are You the Christ? The Trial Narrative in the Gospel of Mark.* Society of Biblical Literature Dissertation Series 10. Missoula MT: Scholar's Press, 1973.

_____. "Introduction: From Passion Traditions to Passion Narrative." In *The Passion in Mark: Studies on Mark 14-16,* ed. Werner H. Kelber, 1-20. Philadelphia: Fortress Press, 1976.

_____. "Jesus as the Parable of God in the Gospel of Mark." *Interpretation* 32 (October 1978): 369-86.

_____. "Miracles, Mystery and Parable." *Way* 18 (1978): 252-62.

_____. "A Neglected Factor in the Theology of Mark." *Journal of Biblical Literature* 101 (December 1982): 563-94.

_____. "Perrin, Norman." In *Dictionary of Biblical Interpretation,* gen. ed. John H. Hayes. Nashville: Abingdon Press, forthcoming 1987-1988.

_____. "Temple, Trial, and Royal Christology (Mark 14:53-65)." In *The Passion in Mark: Studies on Mark 14-16,* ed. Werner H. Kelber, 61-79. Philadelphia: Fortress Press, 1976.

Duling, Dennis. "Interpreting the Markan Hodology." *Nexus* 17 (1974): 2-11.

_____. "Norman Perrin and the Kingdom of God: Review and Response." *Journal of Religion* 64 (October 1984): 468-83.

_____, and Norman Perrin. *The New Testament: An Introduction— Proclamation and Parenesis, Myth and History,* 2nd ed. New York: Harcourt Brace Jovanovich, 1982 [1974].

Ebeling, Gerhard. *Word and Faith,* trans. W. Lestch. Philadelphia: Fortress Press, 1963 [1960].

Frye, Northrup. *Anatomy of Criticism: Four Essays.* New York: Atheneum, 1966 [1957].

Fuchs, Ernst. *Hermeneutik,* 2nd ed. Bad Cannstatt: R. Müllerschön Verlag, 1958 [1954].

_____. *Studies of the Historical Jesus,* trans. Andrew Scobie. London: SCM Press, 1964 [1960].

The Fugitive: A Journal of Poetry 1-4 (1922-25).

Fuller, Reginald H. *A Critical Introduction to the New Testament*. Naperville IL: Alec R. Allenson, 1966.

Funk, Robert W. "The Good Samaritan as Metaphor." *Semeia* 2 (1974): ed. John D. Crossan.

_____. "The Hermeneutical Problem and Literary Criticism." In *The New Hermeneutic*, ed. James Cobb and James M. Robinson, 164-97. New York: Harper and Row, 1964.

_____. *Jesus as Precursor*. Society of Biblical Literature *Semeia* Supplements 2, ed. William A. Beardslee. Philadelphia: Fortress Press, 1975.

_____. *Language, Hermeneutic, and Word of God: The Problem of Language in the New Testament and Contemporary Theology*. New York: Harper and Row, 1966.

_____. "Literary Critical Studies of Biblical Texts." *Semeia* 8 (1977), ed. Robert W. Funk.

_____. *Parables and Presence: Forms of the New Testament Tradition*. Philadelphia: Fortress Press, 1982.

Furnish, Victor P. "Notes on a Pilgrimage: Norman Perrin and New Testament Christology." In *Christology and a Modern Pilgrimage: A Discussion with Norman Perrin*, ed. Hans. Dieter Betz, 92-112. Claremont: Scholar's Press, 1971.

Glicksberg, Charles I., ed. *American Literary Criticism: 1900-1950*. New York: Hendricks House, 1951.

Goss, James. "Eschatology, Autonomy, and Individuation: The Evocative Power of the Kingdom." *Journal of the American Academy of Religion* 49 (September 1981): 363-81.

Grässer, Eric. "Norman Perrin's Contribution to the Question of the Historical Jesus." *Journal of Religion* 64 (October 1984): 484-500.

Harnack, Adolf von. *What is Christianity?* 3rd ed., trans. Thomas Bailey Saunders. New York: G. P. Putnam's Sons, 1912 [1900].

Harvey, Van A. *The Historian and the Believer*. New York: Macmillan, 1966.

Hiers, Richard H. *Jesus and the Future: Unresolved Questions for Understanding and Faith*. Atlanta: John Knox Press, 1981.

_____. *The Kingdom of God in the Synoptic Tradition*. Gainesville: University of Florida Press, 1970.

Hirsch, E. D., Jr. *Validity in Interpretation*. New Haven: Yale University Press, 1967.

Jaspers, Karl and Rudolf Bultmann. *Myth and Christianity*, trans. N. Gutermann. New York: Noonday Press, 1958 [1953, 1954].

Jeremias, Joachim. *The Eucharistic Words of Jesus*, trans. Norman Perrin. London: SCM Press, 1966 [1955].

_____. *The Lord's Prayer*, trans. John Reumann. Philadelphia: Fortress Press, 1964 [1962].

_____. *Jesus' Promise to the Nations*, trans. S. H. Hooke. Studies in Biblical Theology. London: SCM Press, 1958 [1956].

_____. *New Testament Theology: The Proclamation of Jesus*, trans. John Bowden. New York: Charles Scribner's Sons, 1971.

_____. *The Parables of Jesus*, 6th ed., trans. S. H. Hooke. New York: Charles Scribner's Sons, 1963 [1947].

_____. *The Prayers of Jesus*, trans. John Bowden, et al. Studies in Biblical Theology second series 6. Naperville IL: Alec R. Allenson, 1967.

_____. "The Present Position in the Controversy Concerning the Problem of the Historical Jesus." *Expository Times* 69 (August 1958): 333-39.

_____. *The Problem of the Historical Jesus*, trans. Norman Perrin. Facet Books, Biblical Series 13. Philadelphia: Fortress Press, 1964 [1960].

_____. *The Sermon on the Mount*, trans. Norman Perrin. London: Athlone Press, 1961 [1957].

_____. *Unknown Sayings of Jesus*, trans. R. H. Fuller. London: SPCK, 1957 [1951].

Jülicher, Adolf. *Die Gleichnisreden Jesu*, 2 vols. Tübingen: J. C. B. Mohr, 1888, 1889.

Jüngel, Eberhard. *Paulus und Jesus*, 3rd ed. Tübingen: J. C. B. Mohr, 1967 [1962].

Kähler, Martin. *The So-called Historical Jesus and the Historic Biblical Christ*, trans. and ed. Carl E. Braaten. Philadelphia: Fortress Press, 1964 [1896].

Käsemann, Ernst. "Blind Alleys in the 'Jesus of History' Controversy," In *New Testament Questions of Today*, trans. W. J. Montague, 23-65. London: SCM Press, 1969 [1965].

_____. "The Problem of the Historical Jesus." In *Essays on New Testament Themes*. Studies in Biblical Theology 41, trans. W. J. Montague, 15-47. London: SCM Press, 1964 [1960].

Keck, Leander E. "Will the Historical-Critical Method Survive? Some Observations." In *Orientation by Disorientation: Studies in Literary Criticism and Biblical Literary Criticism*, ed. Richard A. Spencer, 115-27. Pittsburgh: Pickwick Press, 1980.

Kelber, Werner H. "The History of the Kingdom in Mark—Aspects of Markan Eschatology." In *The Society of Biblical Literature One Hundred Eighth Annual Meeting Book of Seminar Papers*, ed. Lane C. McGaughy, 1:63-96. Society of Biblical Literature, 1972.

_____, Anitra Bingham Kalenkow, and Robin Scroggs. "Reflections on the Question: Was there a Pre-Markan Passion Narrative?" In *The Society of Biblcal Literature One Hundred Seventh Annual Meeting Seminar Papers* 1:503-85. Society of Biblical Literature, 1971.

_____. *The Kingdom in Mark: A New Place and a New Time*. Philadelphia: Fortress Press, 1974.

_____. "Mark and Oral Tradition." *Semeia* 16 (1979): 7-55.

_____. *Mark's Story of Jesus.* Philadelphia: Fortress Press, 1979.

_____. *The Oral and Written Gospel: The Hermeneutics of Speaking and Writing in the Synoptic Tradition, Mark, Paul, and Q.* Philadelphia: Fortress Press, 1983.

_____, ed. *The Passion in Mark: Studies on Mark 14-16.* Philadelphia: Fortress Press, 1976.

_____. "Redaction Criticism: On the Nature and Exposition of the Gospels." *Perspectives in Religious Studies* 6 (1979): 4-16.

_____. "The Work of Norman Perrin: An Intellectual Pilgrimage." *Journal of Religion* 64 (October 1984): 452-67.

Kissenger, Warren S. *The Parables of Jesus: A History of Interpretation and Bibliography.* ATLA Bibliography Series 4. Metuchen NJ: Scarecrow Press and American Theological Library Association, 1979.

Koester, Helmut. "The Historical Jesus: Some Comments and Thoughts on Norman Perrin's *Rediscovering the Teaching of Jesus.*" In *Christology and a Modern Pilgimage: A Discussion with Norman Perrin,* ed. Hans Dieter Betz, 123-36. Claremont: Scholar's Press, 1971.

_____, and James M. Robinson. *Trajectories Through Early Christianity.* Philadelphia: Fortress Press, 1971.

Kümmel, Werner G. *The New Testament: The History of the Investigation of Its Problems,* trans. S. McLean Gilmour and Howard Clark Kee. Nashville: Abingdon Press, 1972 [1958].

_____. *Promise and Fulfilment: The Eschatological Message of Jesus,* 3rd ed., trans. Dorothea M. Barton. Studies in Biblical Theology 23. Naperville IL: Alec R. Allenson, 1956.

Linnemann, Eta. *Jesus of the Parables: Introduction and Exposition,* 3rd ed. New York: Harper and Row, 1966 [1961].

Lündstrom, Gösta. *The Kingdom of God in the Teaching of Jesus: A History of Interpretation from the Last Decades of the Nineteenth Century to the Present Day,* trans. Joan Bulman. Richmond VA: John Knox Press, 1963 [1947].

Mabee, Charles. *Reimagining America: A Theological Critique of the American Mythos and Biblical Hermeneutics.* Studies in American Biblical Hermeneutics 1. Macon GA: Mercer University Press, 1985.

McKnight, Edgar V. *The Bible and the Reader: An Introduction to Literary Criticism.* Philadelphia: Fortress Press, 1985.

_____. *Meaning in Texts: The Historical Shaping of a Narrative Hermeneutics.* Philadelphia: Fortress Press, 1978.

_____. "Structure and Meaning in Biblical Narrative." *Perspectives in Religious Studies* 3 (Spring 1976): 4-20.

_____. *What is Form Criticism?* Guides to Biblical Scholarship, ed. Dan O. Via, Jr. Philadelphia: Fortress Press, 1969.

Manson, T. W. "The Life of Jesus: Some Tendencies in Present-Day Research." In *The Background of the New Testament and Its Eschatology*, 211-21, ed. W. D. Davies and David Daube. Cambridge: University Press, 1964 [1956].

_____. *The Sayings of Jesus*. London: SCM Press, 1949 [1937].

_____. *The Servant-Messiah: A Study of the Public Ministry of Jesus*. Grand Rapids MI: Baker Book House, 1953.

_____. *The Teaching of Jesus: Studies of Its Form and Content*, 2nd ed. Cambridge: Cambridge University Press, 1955 [1935].

"A Memorial Tribute to Norman Perrin: 1920-1976." *Criterion* 16 (Winter 1977).

Mercer, Calvin R. "Norman Perrin's Pilgrimage: Releasing the Bible to the Public." *The Christian Century* 103 (14 May 1986): 483-86.

Neill, Stephen. *The Interpretation of the New Testament: 1861-1961*. London: Oxford University Press, 1964.

Ogden, Schubert. *Christ Without Myth: A Study Based on the Theology of Rudolf Bultmann*. New York: Harper and Brothers, 1961.

_____. "Debate on Demythologizing." *Journal of Bible and Religion* 27 (January 1959): 17-27.

Petersen, Norman R. *Literary Criticism for New Testament Critics*. Guides to Biblical Scholarship, ed. Dan O. Via, Jr. Philadelphia: Fortress Press, 1978.

Poland, Lynn. *Literary Criticism and Biblical Hermeneutics: A Critique of Formalist Approaches*. American Academy of Religion Academy Series 48, ed. Carl A. Raschke. Chico CA: Scholars Press, 1985.

Ransom, John Crowe *The New Criticism*. Norfolk CT: New Directions, 1941.

_____. *The World's Body*. New York: Charles Scribner's Sons, 1938.

Richards, I. A. *Practical Criticism: A Study of Literary Judgment*. New York: Harcourt, Brace and World, 1929.

Ricoeur, Paul. *Essays on Biblical Interpretation*, ed. Lewis S. Mudge. Philadelphia: Fortress Press, 1980.

_____. "From Proclamation to Narrative." *Journal of Religion* 64 (October 1984): 501-512.

_____. "The Hermeneutics of Symbols and Philosophical Reflection" (1962), trans. Denis Savage. In *The Philosophy of Paul Ricoeur: An Anthology of His Work*, ed. Charles E. Reagan and David Stewart. Boston: Beacon Press, 1978.

_____. *Interpretation Theory: Discourse and the Surplus of Meaning*. Fort Worth: Texas Christian University Press, 1976.

_____. *The Symbolism of Evil*. Boston: Beacon Press, 1969.

Ritschl, Albrecht. *The Christian Doctrine of Justification and Sanctification*, 2nd ed., trans. A. B. Macaulay, ed. H. R. Mackintosh. Edinburgh: T. and T. Clark, 1902 [1847].

Robbins, Vernon K. "The Christology of Mark." Ph.D. Dissertation, University of Chicago Divinity School, 1969.

_____. *Jesus the Teacher: A Socio-Rhetorical Interpretation of Mark.* Philadelphia: Fortress Press, 1984.

_____. "Last Meal: Preparation, Betrayal, and Absence (Mark 14:53-54, 66-72)." In *The Passion of Mark: Studies on Mark 14-16,* 21-40. Philadelphia: Fortress Press, 1976.

_____. "Mark as Genre." In *Society of Biblical Literature 1980 Seminar Papers,* ed. Paul J. Achtemeier, 371-99. Chico CA: Scholar's Press, 1980.

_____. "Pronouncement Stories and Jesus' Blessing of the Children: A Rhetorical Approach." *Semeia* 29 (1983): 42-74.

Robinson, James M. "Hermeneutics Since Barth." In *The New Hermeneutic,* ed. James Cobb and James M. Robinson, 1-77. New York: Harper & Row, 1964.

_____. *A New Quest of the Historical Jesus.* Studies in Biblical Theology 25. Naperville IL: Alec R. Allenson, 1959.

_____. *A New Quest of the Historical Jesus and Other Essays.* Philadelphia: Fortress Press, 1983.

_____. "The Recent Debate on the New Quest." *Journal of Bible and Religion* 30 (July 1962): 198-208.

Sanders, E. P. *Jesus and Judaism.* Philadelphia: Fortress Press, 1985.

Schmidt, Karl Ludwig. *Der Rahmen der Geschichte Jesu.* Berlin: Trowitzsch und Sohn, 1919.

Schweitzer, Albert. *The Mystery of the Kingdom of God: The Secret of Jesus' Messiahship and Passion,* trans. Walter Lowrie. New York: Macmillan, 1950 [1901].

_____. *The Quest of the Historical Jesus: A Critical Study of Its Progress from Reimarus to Wrede,* trans. W. Montgomery. New York: Macmillan, 1968 [1906].

Seal, Welton Ollie, Jr. "Norman Perrin and His 'School,' Retracing a Pilgrimage." *Journal for the Study of the New Testament* 20 (1984): 87-107.

_____. "The Parousia in Mark: A Debate with Norman Perrin and His School." Ph.D. dissertation, Union Theological Seminary, New York, 1982.

Strauss, David F. *The Life of Jesus, Critically Examined,* 4th ed., ed. Peter C. Hodgson, trans. George Eliot. Philadelphia: Fortress Press, 1972.

Suter, David W. *Tradition and Composition in the Parables of Enoch.* Society of Biblical Literature Dissertation Series 47, ed. Howard Clark Kee and Douglas A. Knight. Missoula MT: Scholars Press, 1979.

Tate, Allen. *Reason as Madness: Critical Essays.* New York: G. P. Putnam's Sons, 1941.

Tolbert, Mary Ann. *Perspectives on the Parables: An Approach to Multiple Interpretation.* Philadelphia: Fortress Press, 1979.

Via, Dan O., Jr. *Kerygma and Comedy in the New Testament: A Structuralist Approach to Hermeneutic*. Philadelphia: Fortress Press, 1975.

_____. "Kingdom and Parable: The Search for a New Grasp of Symbol, Metaphor, and Myth." *Interpretation* 31 (April 1977): 181-83.

_____. "Parable and Example Story: A Literary-Structuralist Approach." *Semeia* 1 (1974): 222-35.

_____. *The Parables: Their Literary and Existential Dimension*. Philadelphia: Fortress Press, 1967.

Weiss, Johannes. *Jesus' Proclamation of the Kingdom of God*, trans. and ed. Richard H. Hiers and David L. Holland. Lives of Jesus. Philadelphia: Fortress Press, 1971 [1892].

Wellek, René, and Austin Warren. *Theory of Literature*, 3rd ed. New York: Harcourt, Brace and World, 1956 [1942].

Wheelwright, Philip. *The Burning Foundation: A Study in the Language of Symbolism*, rev. ed. Bloomington: Indiana University Press, 1968 [1954].

_____. *Metaphor and Reality*. Bloomington: Indiana University Press, 1962.

Wilder, Amos N. *Early Christian Rhetoric: The Language of the Gospel*, rev. ed. Cambridge MA: Harvard University Press, 1971 [1964].

_____. "An Experimental Journal for Biblical Criticism: An Introduction." *Semeia* 1 (1974): 1-16.

_____. "The Word as Address and the Word as Meaning." In *The New Hermeneutic*, ed. James Cobb and James M. Robinson, 198-218. New York: Harper and Row, 1964.

Wrede, Wilhelm. *The Messianic Secret*, trans. J. C. G. Greig. Cambridge: Clarke, 1971 [1901].

·INDEXES·

· Index of Principal Subjects ·

• Index of Authors •

• Index of Ancient Texts •